Ancient Celtic Legends: The History of Celtic Folk Tales and Myths that Influenced European Mythology

By Char

An illustration of Cuchulainn carrying Ferdiad

About Charles River Editors

Charles River Editors provides superior editing and original writing services across the digital publishing industry, with the expertise to create digital content for publishers across a vast range of subject matter. In addition to providing original digital content for third party publishers, we also republish civilization's greatest literary works, bringing them to new generations of readers via ebooks.

Sign up here to receive updates about free books as we publish them, and visit Our Kindle Author Page to browse today's free promotions and our most recently published Kindle titles.

Introduction

A sculpture of a Celtic warrior

"Throughout all of Gaul there are two classes of people who are treated with dignity and honor. This does not include the common people, who are little better than slaves and never have a voice in councils. Many of these align themselves with a patron voluntarily, whether because of debt or heavy tribute or out of fear of retribution by some other powerful person. Once they do this, they have given up all rights and are scarcely better than servants. The two powerful classes mentioned above are the Druids and the warriors. Druids are concerned with religious matters, public and private sacrifices, and divination." – Julius Caesar

The Celts are one of the most well-known groups in Europe and one of the least understood. Depending on which classifications are used, the Celts are also one of the oldest civilizations in Europe. In the centuries before Christ, the Celts were spread out across much of continental Europe, and though they are mostly identified with Gaul, evidence suggests they also spread as far as Portugal. Though they were spread out across Europe before the height of the Roman Empire, most people associate the Celts with the British Isles today, particularly Ireland and Scotland. After they had been relegated to those smaller regions as a result of the Romans and other migrations, the culture of the Celts as it is currently understood began to congeal during the Early Middle Ages, and Celtic culture, folklore, and legend have all become inextricably intertwined with Irish history and British history as a whole.

Historically, Celtic cultures differ from their English and French neighbors in a number of ways, including social organization, language, values and economic systems, but one of the most captivating of these has always been their myths. Celtic Myths, which can be read in translation without needing special training in grammar, are more accessible than the Celtic languages, and unlike the other distinctive features that have faded over the centuries, myths still have their immediacy and power when read today. While much has undoubtedly been lost from the ancient Celts over time, medieval manuscripts help scholars understand how Celtic myths have reached the form they have today. Like many ancient belief systems, Celtic mythology shares Indo-European roots, meaning Celtic beliefs have cousins in related societies like the Norse, Greeks, Romans and Slavs, with a foundation of shared mythmaking that goes back several millennia. Descriptions of Celtic mythology by their contemporaries, including the Ancient Romans and Greeks, provide a hazy picture, while the tales recorded by Christian monks and undoubtedly bear the stamp of their own religious affiliations.

Ancient Celtic Legends: The History of Celtic Folk Tales and Myths that Influenced European Mythology

About Charles River Editors

Introduction

    The Ancient Celts and Their Religious Roots

    The Celtic Pantheon

    Archaeological Links to Celtic Mythology

    The Druids

    Christianity

    The Impact on Britannia

    Legends in Other Celtic Lands

    Celtic Heritage

    Further Reading

The Ancient Celts and Their Religious Roots

When someone is talking about the "Celts", there are a number of different things he or she could be talking about. In its strictest definition, "Celtic" describes a small family of languages found in the northwestern fringes of Europe, and the "Celts" are the people who use those languages or are descended from people who do. However, due to the passage of time and the mingling of cultures, much that is described as "Celtic" has nothing to do with language and can be only connected tangentially to the speakers of languages like Cornish, Manx and Breton. As a result, some scholars (in particular, those following the lead of Malcolm Chapman[1]) dismiss the very idea of "Celts" as a fantasy which the English used to categorize, control and dismiss the relevance of the people who lived in the fringes of their state, particularly the Irish but also the Scottish Highlanders and Welsh. Not surprisingly, this position has been vigorously rejected by those who consider themselves Celts today.[2]

While the writings of the Celto-skeptics are interesting, many scholars do subscribe to the belief that there is such a thing as the Celtic Language family, and that the people who spoke these languages do have historic and cultural similarities, even if many of the similarities were due to their marginal position under the English state. With that said, geneticists and Celtic nationalists have attempted to find a genetic link amongst Celtic peoples for a long time, but ultimately they have only had limited success. This is largely due to the fact that language is not passed along bloodlines, and huge populations can dramatically change language within a few generations, such as the descendants of Africans who speak Portuguese in Brazil or the descendants of Chinese immigrants who speak English or Spanish in the Americas. Thus, while scholars can potentially trace the linguistic origins and history of the Celtic peoples, there is no way to ensure that any genetic research done upon today's Celts will provide accurate information about ancient users of that language family.

---

[1] Chapman has written a number of works, but the most important is *The Celts: The Construction of a Myth*, published in 1993 by St. Martin's Press.
[2] For example, see the essay, "Do the Celts Exist?" by Craig Weatherhill, accessed online at http://breselyerkeltic.com/do-the-celts-exist-by-craig-weatherhill/

The yellow area represents the Celtic presence in the 6th century B.C. The lighter shades of green represent the expansion of the Celts in the 3rd century B.C. The dark green represents the Six Celtic Nations and areas where the Celtic languages are still spoken today.

For decades, scholars, linguists and archaeologists have sought to fuse information culled from the surviving Celtic languages, the physical remains of the past, and historic documents to reconstruct the lives and histories of the various Celtic peoples. The historical search begins by examining language. While people often think of language as constantly changing, with new slang words appearing seemingly by the day, there are many elements of language that are quite conservative and slow to change. These parts include pronunciation, grammar and "basic core vocabulary" (like pronouns, parts of the body and family relations). Basic core vocabulary changes so slowly that linguists can use it to compare and contrast languages and look for ancient links between them. Because changes to these words accumulate not only slowly but also at a relatively regular rate, linguists can compare two branches of a related language tree (like Italian and Spanish) and estimate at what point the two languages diverged from one another. This is a rough estimate, but for particularly ancient divisions, before the invention of writing, it is often the best date available. This process is known as glottochronology.

Almost all European, Iranian and Indian languages descend from a single language called "Proto-Indo-European."[3] For example, linguists have attempted to reconstruct Proto-Indo-European (PIE), and by using some clever comparison and backtracking, they have argued that the concept of the word "around" was originally spoken in PIE as something like *ambi-**[4].

---

[3] European exceptions include Basque, Finnish, Hungarian, Estonian, Saami, Turkish and Gagauz.
[4] Linguists use an asterisk (*) to mark a word that they have reconstructed but have no hard evidence for.

Linguists have found Gaulish examples from modern-day France and Celtoiberian from modern-day Spain that use the term *ambi-* almost identically. In the contemporary Old Irish, which also has written examples, linguists have found the use of *imm-* and the use of am- in Middle Welsh. This pattern also continued into the present day: in modern Scots Gaelic *im-*, in Welsh *am-, em-* or *ym-*, in Breton *am-* or *em-* and in Cornish *am-, ym-, om-* or *em-*. It is apparent that the terms resemble each other, and that their variations have slowly shifted over time.[5]

There are considerable debates amongst linguists as to when and where Proto-Indo-European emerged and began to break into today's language families, with some arguing modern-day Turkey around 8,700 years ago[6] and others the southern Russian Steppes around 6,000 years ago[7]. Regardless, the language communities that would eventually speak Celtic broke from this mother tongue many thousands of years ago and moved westward into what is now Central Europe, where the language emerged into a form that is recognized as distinctly Celtic.

---

[5]"Examples from the Celtic Core Vocabulary." Accessed online at: http://www.wales.ac.uk/Resources/Documents/Research/CelticLanguages/ExamplesCelticCoreVocabulary.PDF

[6]"Early date for the birth of Indo-European languages" by Michael Balter for the journal *Science*, (Nov 28, 2003): 1490-1.

[7]*The Horse, the Wheel, and Language: How Bronze-Age Riders from the Eurasian Steppes Shaped the Modern World*, by David W. Anthony (2007). Princeton University Press

A Celtic stele from around the 2nd century A.D.

Within the language family, recent research indicates that the northern Goidelic Celtic languages (Irish, Scots Gaelic and Manx) broke off from the southern Brythonic languages (Welsh, Cornish and Breton) around 1100 B.C. The Continental Celtic, usually referred to as the extinct language of Gaulish, separated from the Brythonic languages around 1000 B.C. The splintering of these subfamilies into the named languages of today happened relatively recently, with the Brythonic languages separating in the 9th century A.D. and the Goidelic in the 8th century A.D.[8]

---

[8] "On the position of Gaulish within Celtic from the point of view of glottochronology" by Václav Blazek in the journal Indogermanische Forschungen #114 (2009): 257-299; "On Application of Glottochronology for Celtic Languages" by Václav Blazek in the journal *Celto-Slavica: Second International Colloquium of Societas Celto-Slavica*. pp. 11-36. 2006, Moskva.

The techniques of historical linguistics, including glottochronology, provide the necessary evidence to link the ancient Celts to various timeperiods. Because much of modern archaeology works to provide links between archaeological discoveries and particular times, linguistic information allows researchers to go one step further and associate a language with archaeological remains as well. If this sounds complex, that's because it is. This task is riddled with the potential for mistakes, and the archaeology of Celtic remains is often a very controversial subject. As a result, in some cases the word "Celt" has been removed and replaced with more neutral terms like "Iron-Age Peoples", to the consternation of many Celtic nationalists. However, the fact that the Celtic languages exist today means that they have existed throughout history, and with them Celtic peoples. In other words, archaeological studies of the Celts are not impossible but merely difficult, and as techniques have become far more refined in recent years, they have provided an increasingly clear picture of the past.

Due to ancient accounts, there has long been a debate over the location and origins of the first Celts. Roman writers like Julius Caesar used the term Celts to refer to people who the Romans came into contact with in France, while ancient Greek historian Herodotus suggested the Celts were originally near the Rhine River. Today, the first group that archaeologists tentatively connect to the Celts is a cultural group called the Urnfield Culture, which existed primarily in today's eastern and southern France and western Germany. They were known for their cremated burials in urns and were considered to be a Bronze Age people, since they used metal tools constructed of bronze, a mixture of copper and tin, and practiced agriculture. The Bronze Age is typically associated with the classic Dynastic Egypt, the empires of Sumer and Babylonia in today's Iraq, the Pre-Classic Greece of Homer and the Minoan civilization of the island of Crete.

An urn constructed sometime during the 10th-8th centuries B.C.

The Urnfield people existed from around 1300-750 B.C. and were expansionist, clearly relying on their impressive hill forts. The division of the main branches of the Celtic languages (set around 1100 B.C.) occurred in this period and may be linked to a series of events around 1200-1100 B.C. that are known as the Bronze Age Collapse. This mysterious time was a period of massive social upheaval, population movements, and societal collapse throughout the Mediterranean, including the collapse of the Hittite Empire and the Egyptian New Kingdom. The Bronze Age Collapse had repercussions throughout Europe, especially if the cause, as some believe, was due to climate change.[9]

---

[9]"Empires in the Dust" by Karen Wright in the magazine *Discover* March, 1998. "The Influence of Climatic Change on the Late Bronze Age Collapse and the Greek Dark Ages" by Brandon L. Drake in the *Journal of Archaeological Science* XXX (2012):1-9

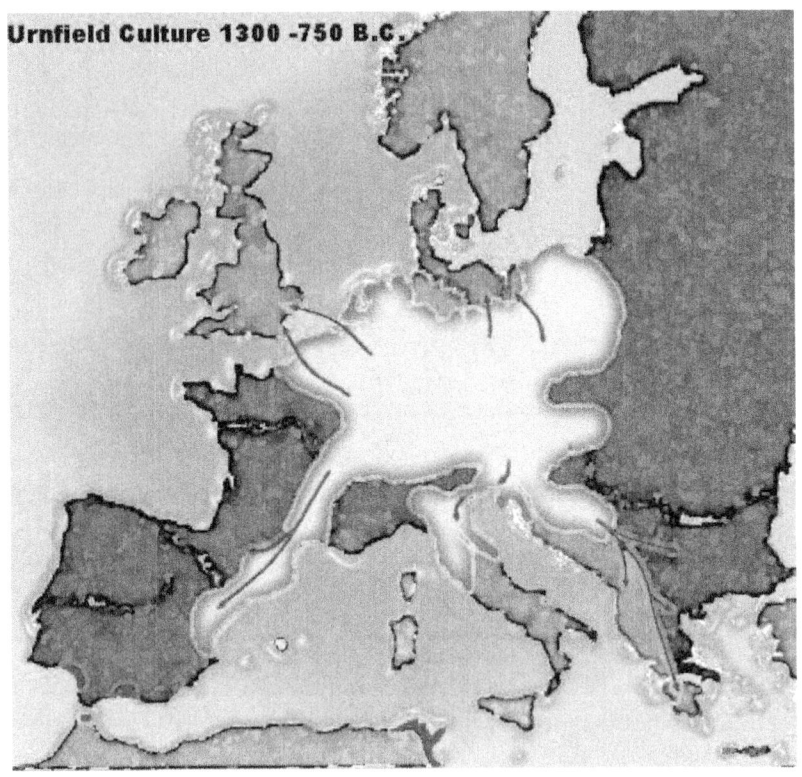

The movements of the Urnfield Culture in yellow from 1300-750 B.C.

Collapses aside, culture change in the archaeological record tends to be a slow process as one "culture" slowly gives way to another. Eventually, the Urnfield people were replaced by a set of cultural remains that archaeologists refer to as the Hallstatt Culture, which thrived from around 900-600 B.C. This was probably not an actual replacement of one group of people by another but an evolution of technology and traditions that saw the old ways remain at the peripheries long after the wealthy areas converted to the new forms. The most noticeable addition was the use of iron tools, which means the Hallstatt are an Iron Age people.

Archaeologists believe that despite a similarity in technology, there are enough differences between the eastern and western branches of the Hallstatt to distinguish them from each other. The eastern branch resided in today's Czech and Slovak republics, parts of the northern former Yugoslavia, and parts of Hungary and Austria, while the western branch was in northern France, parts of northern Switzerland, Bavaria, Northern Italy, and the northern parts of Spain and Portugal.

The Hallstat (orange) in 800 B.C. and their expansion (tan) by 500 B.C.

The western branch is typically associated with the Celtic peoples, while the east is associated with another Indo-European group called the Illyrians[10]. In the west, the people used and were even occasionally buried with mighty chariots, and they built hilltop forts like their predecessors. While the easterners began to trade with Greece early, the western (presumably Celtic) Hallstatt people only came into regular contact with the Mediterranean trade routes after 600 B.C.[11] This is important for two reasons. The first is that the control of luxury goods from these areas was apparently a key element in the rise of more centralized government (which are now called "chiefdoms"). Second, it was these Mediterranean peoples who possessed writing and thus began to document the existence of the peoples related to the ancient Celts.

Entering the 5th century B.C., scholars are able to draw more concrete connections between people, place and language based on all three forms of documentation: linguistic analysis of language fragments, archaeology of sites, and the written records of ancient observers, most importantly the Romans. The group that emerged out of the Hallstatt people, known in archaeological circles as the "La Tène" culture, has been directly linked to the Celts of Roman history. This was perhaps the Golden Age of the Celtic peoples, who were at the height of their

---

[10] The Illyrians are potentially the linguistic ancestors of today's Albanians. For more information on the theory, see *The Illyrians to the Albanians* by Neritan Ceka (2005), Publishing House Migjeni. Certainly, the Albanians speak a form of Indo-European as distinct from others (and therefore as ancient) as the Celtic family is from the Germanic.

[11] "Hallstatt Culture" in *Cassell's Peoples, Nations and Cultures (2005)*. Retrieved from http://www.credoreference.com.libezproxy2.syr.edu/entry/orionpnc/hallstatt_culture

military power and artistic endeavors and were spread out as far as they ever would.

Reconstruction of a La Tène settlement in Germany

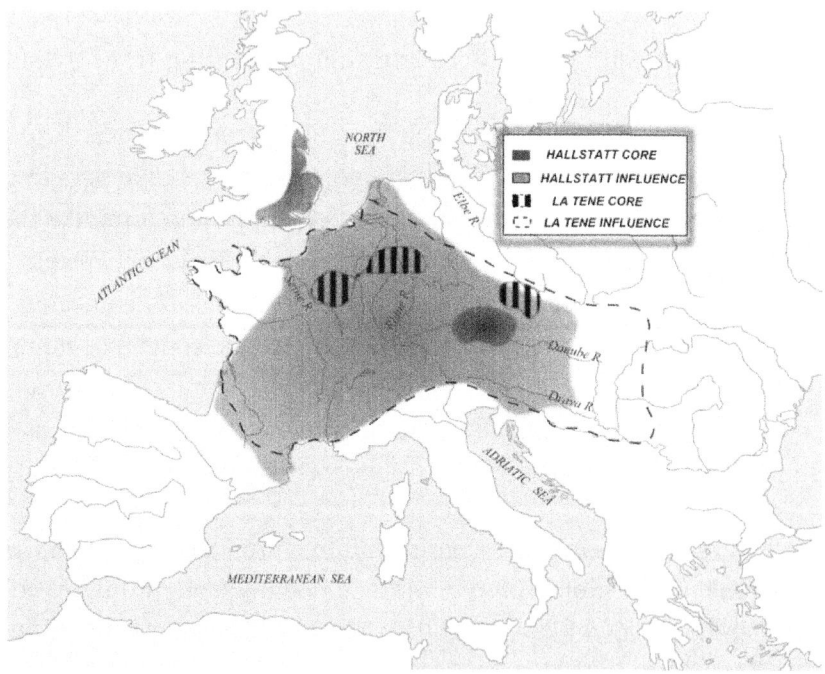

The heartland of their influence was in what is now France and southern Germany, where they were referred to as "Gauls" and their language was called "Gaulish." In Spain, they were known as the Celtiberians, after they arrived during the twilight of the Hallstatt period (the 6th and 7th centuries B.C.) and occupied the Ebro Valley the in northeastern area of Spain. The Celtiberians were documented by Roman writers like the geographer Strabo, who noted that they were known to the classical Greeks. It is also believed that Herodotus was referring to the Celtiberians when he talked about the Celts living "beyond the pillars of Hercules" The 4th century B.C. Greek poet Ephorus wrote that they had "the same customs as the Greeks." It was likely the Greeks who first labeled people Kelts, and their other references to Iberians likely led to their compounding of the names into Keltiberians, thus ignorantly uniting various distinct nations.[12] The Romans didn't make much of a distinction either, though Strabo did note differences between the peoples in Germany and the Iberian Peninsula, writing, "Now the parts beyond the Rhenus, immediately after the country of the Celti, slope towards the east and are occupied by the Germans, who, though they vary slightly from the Celtic stock in that they are wilder, taller, and have yellower hair, are in all other respects similar, for in build, habits, and modes of life they are such as I have said the Celti are. And I also think that it was for this reason that the Romans assigned to them the name "Germani," as though they wished to indicate thereby that they were 'genuine' Galatae, for in the language of the Romans 'germani' means 'genuine.'"

The Celts were drawn further into the Mediterranean world by allying themselves with the Carthaginians in the Punic Wars, which is not altogether surprising since Hannibal and his father had established Carthaginian power in southern Spain. However, it proved to be a big mistake after Carthage's total defeat at the hands of the Romans; naturally, the Romans had little sympathy for the Celtiberians as they moved to dominate the Iberian Peninsula.[13] Strabo wrote in his seminal *Geography*, "As for Iberia, the Romans did not stop reducing it by force of arms until they had subdued the whole of it, first, by driving out the Nomantini, and, later on, by destroying Viriathus and Sertorius, and, last of all, the Cantabri, who were subdued by Augustus Caesar. As for Celtica (I mean Celtica as a whole, both the Cisalpine and Transalpine, together with Liguria), the Romans at first brought it over to their side only part by part, from time to time, but later the Deified Caesar, and afterwards Caesar Augustus, acquired it all at once in a general war. But at the present time the Romans are carrying on war against the Germans, setting out from the Celtic regions as the most appropriate base of operations, and have already glorified the fatherland with some triumphs over them."

The greater concentration of Celts was, however, further north in today's France. These Gauls developed the art style that is today known throughout the world as "Celtic": curvilinear 'S' shaped designs with complex symmetrical geometric patterns. Some surviving pieces include the bronze Battersea Shield, the Waterloo Helmet and the Wandsworth Shield, all kept at the British Museum in London.[14] The Celts of this period were known for their aristocratic warrior class, which rode to battle in chariots wearing spectacular armor. With that said, their territories, which stretched from the British Islands, through France and Germany, east into the Czech

---

[12] This is from Strabo's *Geography* 1:2:27. This translation is from the edition for Bohn's Classical Library, translated by H.C. Hamilton, Esq (1854).

[13] "Celtiberians" in *Cassell's Peoples, Nations and Cultures (2005)*. Retrieved from http://www.credoreference.com.libezproxy2.syr.edu/entry/orionpnc/celtiberians

[14] "Explore: The Battersea Shield" at the homepage of the British Museum. Accessed online at http://www.britishmuseum.org/explore/highlights/highlight_objects/pe_prb/t/the_battersea_shield.aspx

Republic, and south into Switzerland and even Italy, were never politically united, and it is unclear whether they had a single ethnic identity. While there were certainly artistic and linguistic links, they were divided into dozens of warring chiefdoms. Moreover, while they were called "Celts" by the Romans, they probably did not think of themselves using those terms.

Despite their divisions, the Celtic leaders were able to mount highly effective military campaigns from their rich heartlands, moving out into Italy and the Balkans in the 3rd and 4th centuries B.C. and reaching as far as modern-day Turkey. Celtic soldiers even sacked the city of Rome in 390 BC. This expansionism was not due to an inherent warlike or emotional nature but to the fact that chiefdom government structures like theirs rewarded conquest as a path for self-promotion. In many ways, their government and social structures were similar to those found around the Mediterranean world in the centuries before the Roman Empire, only that the Celts were particularly effective at utilizing those structures for their own benefit.[15]

Much of what is known about the Continent Celts in this period comes from surviving writings, in particular those of the Romans and Greeks who fought against the Celts throughout that era. Of course, much of the writing takes on the tone of propaganda and is laden with descriptions of drunken, barbaric Celts without the marks of civilization that the Romans and Greeks saw in themselves.[16] Reading about a culture from its enemies is always a tricky business, but after the Roman Empire conquered Gaul (and Iberia) by the 1st century A.D., the Gaulish or "Gallic" Celts were integrated en-masse into Roman culture. While the French state classically likes to refer to "Our Ancestors the Gauls" in the 19th century, little remains of their language or culture in contemporary France, even though a shared Celtic past remains a symbolically potent idea.[17]

With the Roman conquest and integration of Gaul, this left the British Isles, which may have possibly been on the Celtic periphery, as the only available land remaining for them. While the Romans would also conquer much of modern-day England, the Celtic presence remained stronger there, especially in unconquered Ireland and Wales.

Unlike Christianity or Buddhism, whose origins can be traced to a singular religious teacher, Celtic mythology - and in fact all Celtic religion - appears to have grown out of ancient folk traditions. While the Celts undoubtedly had major theologians, prophets and similar figures,

---

[15] "La Tène." *Encyclopædia Britannica. Encyclopædia Britannica Online Academic Edition.* Encyclopædia Britannica Inc., 2013. Web. 15 Mar. 2013.
  <http://www.britannica.com.libezproxy2.syr.edu/EBchecked/topic/326554/La-Tene>.
[16] "The Ancient Celts" In *Cassell's Peoples, Nations and Cultures (2005)*. Retrieved from http://www.credoreference.com.libezproxy2.syr.edu/entry/orionpnc/celts_ancient
[17] "Our Ancestors the Gauls: Archaeology, Ethnic Nationalism and the Manipulation of Celtic Identity in Modern Europe" by Michael Dietler (1994) in the journal *American Anthropologist* 96(3):584-605.

they are lost to time, so in this way, Celtic myth is similar to the traditions of Indian Hinduism or Japanese Shinto, which have also evolved over millennia. Thus, when scholars have inquired about the ultimate origins of the figures of Celtic myth, they have turned to an even more shadowy ancient tradition they call the Indo-Europeans.

According to the theory (which has widespread support among academics but can never be completely proven), the vast majority of the linguistic and mythological systems of Europe, Iran and India[18] can be traced by to an ancient Central Asian nomadic group called the "Indo-Europeans," who eventually expanded into both Europe and Asia and probably converted many peoples to their cultural traditions. In the same way these people influenced all the languages, they also influenced religion, so it is possible to understand something about Celtic mythology by comparing it to neighboring faiths and tracing back the shared Indo-European roots.

All of the Indo-Europeans were polytheistic peoples, in contrast with monotheism (the worship of one god) or henotheism (the worship of one god but the belief that other gods exist). One example of an inheritance from this truly ancient religion included a god of hammers, thunder and alcohol worshiped by the ancient Gauls named "Taranis". Taranis was related to similar hammer gods, including Thor (among the Norse), Perkunas (among the Lithuanians), and Perun (among the Slavs)[19]. Another god that potentially had Indo-European roots was Nechtan, a god of the sea who shared an origin with other aquatic deities like Poseidon (among the Greeks), Nethuns (of the Etruscans) and the German water spirit Nix. Undoubtedly, there were similar connections amongst numerous ancient gods which have been lost to time.

---

18 The large exceptions in the areas discussed would include the Finns and Balts, the Turks, the Basques, the Arabs and the Dravidian languages of India.
19 *Thor: The Origins, Evolution and History of the Norse God* by Jesse Harasta (2013). Charles Rivers Editors.

A figurine depicting Taranis.

Perhaps the most important potential ancient Indo-European inheritance into the Celtic religion, one that potentially continues to resonate today, is the concept of a triple goddess. There are several Celtic myths that relate to a deity which is both three and one simultaneously. Perhaps the best known is the Morrigan; appearing in Irish myth, the Morrigan is a goddess with three aspects. One is the Morrigan herself, a warrior goddess who also patronizes fertility and general conflict. At the same time, she is also connected to two other goddesses: Babd ("Crow") and another being named either Macha (also "Crow") or Namain (which means "Frenzy")[20]. Scholars have found carvings in Celtic Gaul and Britain from the period of Roman

---

20 "The Morrigan" at the *Encyclopedia Mythica* (1997). Accessed online at:

occupation depicting an apparent protective triple deity called the "Hooded Spirits" (or "Cuculatti"), which appear to be associated with fertility and healing[21]. The Morrigan and the Hooded Spirits are dramatic examples of a common motif in religions that descend from the Indo-European tree, and non-Celtic examples include the Greek Fates, their Norse equivalent (the Norns), the Matres of Rome, and the Zoryas (the three sky goddesses of the eastern Slavs).[22] It has been argued that when St. Patrick came to Ireland to convert the pagan Irish, he used their familiarity with the concept of a Triple God and the three-leaf clover to teach the concept of the Christian[23] Holy Trinity.[24] Another possible continuance of the Triple Goddess theme are the Three Queens who brought the dying King Arthur to Avalon to await rebirth.

What these examples demonstrate is researchers' ability to understand some of the earliest roots of the Celtic myths as emerging from a shared Indo-European source, which also inspired much of the mythology of the Greeks, Romans, Norse, Slavs and other peoples. These shadowy foundations will never be much clearer than they are now, but they offer the best look into the distant past.

The Celtic Pantheon

One school of thought holds that some of the ancient myths and legends are based on real people and events. The stories people are told are merely the imperfect translations about those personalities and events through the lens of a primitive people who did not possess the proper vocabulary to describe what had happened.

For instance, the Greek myth of the centaur may merely have been the startled disbelief of primitives who had never seen men on horseback. Their befuddled minds saw the human head, arms, and torso, but ignored the horse's head. They saw the horse's legs, but did not recognize the human legs, perhaps wrapped in leather leggings and boots.

So, what can we make of the chief Celtic goddess and the lesser gods and goddesses? Like the pantheons of the Greeks and Romans, the Celt gods and goddesses had many traits that make them out to be much like any multi-talented human, or any competent leader who has numerous

---

    http://www.pantheon.org/articles/m/morrigan.html
21 "The Hooded Spirits" at the Encyclopedia *Mythica* (1997). Accessed online at: http://www.pantheon.org/articles/h/hooded_spirits.html; "Cuculatti" at the *Mythology Dictionary* (2014). Accessed online at: http://www.mythologydictionary.com/Cuculatti-mythology.html
22 "Zorya" by Anthony E. Smart at the *Encyclopedia Mythica* (1997). Accessed online at: http://www.pantheon.org/articles/z/zorya.html
23 While the Holy Trinity is a triple god, like those described above, Christianity is not an Indo-European religion, but instead emerges out of the Semitic religions of the Near East, which include Judaism, Islam, Samaritanism, Druze and the lost faiths of Babylon, Canaan, and Sumer. That said, the Trinity only entered Christianity *after* it had been adopted by Indo-European speaking Greeks and Romans and it - like the Immaculate Conception - may have been a borrowed concept.
24 "St. Patrick" at the *Catholic Encyclopedia* at the *New Advent* website. Accessed online at: http://www.newadvent.org/cathen/11554a.htm

interests. For instance, the Apollo of both Greek and Roman pantheons was not only a god of the Sun, but also of archery, dance and music, prophecy and truth, healing and diseases, poetry, and others. And, like the challenges of translation between languages, an exact match between pantheons proves difficult.

The following gods and goddesses are either the chief Celtic deities or simply those which were known from evidence across more than one region.

Anextlomarus - Compared to Roman's Apollo. Literally: "great protector." Inscriptions found in northern France, northern Britain, and in Switzerland at Aventicum (Avenches). The Swiss inscription is spelled "Anextlomara."

Anu (alternately, Ana or Anann) - "The mother of all Irish gods," according to the Bishop Cormac Glossary. While this fertility goddess was special to the people of Munster, the whole of Ireland has been called, in the ancient, epic poetry, the "Land of Anu." This may also be an earlier version of Danu - the namesake of the Tuatha Dé Danann. It is interesting to note that the Etruscan pantheon included the goddess of "beginnings" named "Ana."

Belenus (alternately Bel, Belinu, Belinus, or Belus) - Compared to the Roman's Apollo. Meaning: "to shine" or "light." Known throughout Celtic Europe with the greatest number of inscriptions found in northern Italy, southern France, and in the eastern region of the Alps. Perhaps the highest concentration was found in Italy at Aquileia. The god seems to have been associated with protection, especially to the tribes of northeast Italy, and with springs of health-giving waters. On the Italian peninsula, inscriptions for this god have been found as far south as Rome and Rimini.

Brigantia (Brigindo in eastern Gaul?) - Romans compared this goddess with their own named Victory. Meaning: "the sublime one." Worship of this goddess seems to have been concentrated in northern England and southern Scotland. A relief pictorial shows the goddess with symbolic ties to Victory and Minerva. One inscription equates her to an African goddess named Caelestis - perhaps Juno Caelestis, the Roman name for the chief Carthaginian goddess named "Tanit."

Brigit (alternately, Brigid) - Skilled in poetry, metalwork, and healing. Daughter of the Dagda. Some scholars speculate that this goddess was derived from the older myth of Brigantia *(which see, above)*.

Camulus - Romans compared to Mars. Worshipped throughout Celtic Europe with inscriptions found in western Germany, southern Belgium, northern France, Scotland, and even in Rome. One inscription included ram's horns with an oak leaf crown. His name was the inspiration for the Roman town of Camulodunum, what today is Colchester, England, in the southeast of the island.

Cernunnos - God of fertility, prosperity, and nature (both fauna and flora). Throughout Europe, he is shown with either stag antlers or horns. Though he is shown having human form, he is frequently depicted with animal legs and hooves, and displayed with legs crossed. Scholars debate whether his name derives from the Celtic word for "antler" or "horn," based on the Indo-European root, "ker," meaning "horn" (rhinoceros, triceratops, and from Celtic-Italic blend, corner, Capricorn, tricorn, unicorn). His name is related to one cultural hero of the Ulster Cycle named Conall Cernach. According to some scholars, he is also the inspiration behind some depictions in Christian art of Satan.

Condatis - A god of the confluence, or "coming together," of two rivers. Several such locations throughout Gaul were named Condates. He was also worshipped in northeastern England, especially between the Tees and Tyne rivers. For some reason, the Romans compared him to Mars, their god of war.

Danu (alternately Dana) - Mother goddess who is specifically mentioned in Irish myth as a leader of the Tuatha Dé Danann. Her name, which means "waters of heaven" or "stream," appears all across Europe in place names, including, it seems, the River Danube.

Epona - Goddess and protector of the horse, known throughout Celtic Europe, with inscriptions found from the Balkans to Iberia. Numerous images of the goddess have survived. Some show her riding side-saddle. Others show her sitting upon a throne while nestling a cornucopia (horn of plenty) or a bowl, and with a horse standing on one side or the other. Still other images include a dog, bird, or foal. Roman writers mentioned her as late as the second century AD. Statues of her were sometimes placed in horse stables.

Grannus - Romans compared this god to Apollo because of his healing powers. Many of the inscriptions use the combined name, Apollo-Grannus. Evidence of his veneration has been found in Hungary, Germany, France, Spain, and the Netherlands. The goddess Sirona was his consort and many of the votive dedications made to this god were also made to her because of their close relationship.

Leucetius (alternately Loucetius) - A god of war with a name meaning "to shine." Evidence of his worship has been found in Bath in southwestern England, Strasbourg in eastern France, and in western Germany.

Lugus (alternately Logos, Lugh, or Lugos) - God of sun, light, wisdom, and omniscience. Some scholars speculate that he is the Celtic god which Julius Caesar portrayed as their chief deity. His name has been used in numerous locations, most notably modern Lyon, formerly known as Lugdunum of southeast Gaul. In later legends, this god is portrayed as both a cultural hero in Ireland and as a great warrior. Some of his nicknames include: Lugh Lámfhota (or Lámfada), which means Lugh "of the long hand" or "the long-armed," based on his skill in launching weapons at his enemies; and Lugh Samildánach, which means Lugh "skilled in many arts and crafts."

In that later mythology, he also led the race of good gods, the Tuatha Dé Danann, to triumph over the evil Fomorians. His forces met that malevolent race of seafaring gods at the Battle of Mag Tuired, where he slew, with his magic spear, Balor the one-eye. And from that victory he established four decades of prosperity and peace.

Maponus (alternately Maponas) - Romans compared him to Apollo. Meaning literally "child" or "son." Inscriptions to this god are found in Chamalières, France, and in northern England. After the Romans conquered the Celts in this region, the god is shown caressing a lyre, like Apollo, and is thus additionally related to poetry and music.

Matronae (alternately Martrae or Matres) - A trio of goddesses known sometimes as mothers or matrons and occasionally as maidens. They were viewed as protectors of family and are shown holding infants, wheat, fruit baskets, or flowers, symbolizing abundance and fertility. Their statues and inscriptions are found throughout Celtic Europe, including Slovenia, Spain, Portugal, Germany, eastern France, and northern Italy. [See also Matrona (France).]

Nemetona - A goddess named after the Celtic word "nemeton," meaning "a sacred grove of trees." Inscriptions have been found in eastern Germany and in England, some of which name her as consort to the Roman god of war, Mars.

Ogmios (alternately, Ogma?) - Though some scholars compare this god with the underworld, there are other indications that he was related more with literacy and eloquence. With regard to the underworld, then, this god would be comparable to Hades (Greek); Dis Pater or Orcus, later merged into Pluto (Roman); and Aita (Etruscan god of endings, opposing Ana, Etruscan goddess of beginnings; both later adopted and merged by the Romans as two-faced Janus, from whom weget our name for January). One writer of the second century AD - Lucian of Samosata - likened him to Hercules. Lucian told of seeing a statue of the god in Gaul. This deity had been portrayed as a senior citizen, dark skin, wearing a lion skin, and holding a club. Along with the statue were statuettes of people made of amber, each one attached to the god by chains coming from the god's tongue and ears. When Lucian inquired about the meaning, the Gallic Celts said that the entire display was a demonstration of "eloquence." So, perhaps the chains did not represent slavery, for the god was not holding them. Instead, they may merely have been lines of communication, with the god giving and receiving well-spoken words. This trait is frequently associated with Mercury (Roman) and Hermes (Greek), the messenger god of the Greco-Roman pantheons. Consistent with this idea, we find in Irish myth from a later time the fact that "Ogma" (an alternate spelling?) had been the one who gave the Celts the art of writing - a function attributed in Egyptian mythology to Thoth from the far West. Curiously, this god's name is found in two curse tablets made of lead, found in Bregenz, Austria.

Olloudius - Though the Romans compared this god to Mars (god of war), one surviving idol found in England shows him wearing a cloak and cap while holding a cornucopia (horn of plenty) and an offering plate. These details do not suggest belligerence, but instead, prosperity, fertility, and perhaps even healing. Inscriptions to this god have been found in southern France and southwest England.

Sucellus (alternately, Sucaelus or Succelus) - Worshipped throughout the continent, he is shown with a beard, short tunic, boots, and a long scepter with what appears to be a hammer head on top. In some depictions, he is accompanied by a dog. On one altar in eastern France, the town of Sarrebourg, he is shown with his consort, the goddess Nantosuelta. In the Gallic Celt language, his name comes from *su-*, a prefix meaning "well" or "good" and from the root word, *cellos,* which has been interpreted to mean "striker," based on the Indo-European root, *kel-do-s,* which has given us Lithuanian *kálti,* meaning "to forge" or "to hammer," Greek *klao,* meaning "to break," and Latin *per-cellere,* meaning "striker." Thus, his name has typically been translated as "good striker."

Suleviae - A set of three sisters worshipped throughout much of the Celtic world, especially in Germany and Britain, but also in Rome, where numerous Celtic mercenaries worked for the empire. The sister goddesses are thought to have been guardians of divine protection and regeneration, two subjects keen to the mind of a warrior.

Teutates (alternately Toutates) - Romans compared him with Mars, god of war. The name seems to be derived from Celtic words meaning "father of the tribe," or "god of the tribe." His votive inscriptions have been found throughout Europe, including Rome, Austria, and Britain. Lucan, the first century AD Roman poet, mentioned that humans sacrificed to this god were dunked headfirst into a container of water and held down until drowned.

Local, Regional, and Minor Celtic Deities

For many of the Celtic gods, we have only limited evidence from one region. It remains quite possible, however, that some of them were worshipped by Celts in a wider array of locations.

British Isles

Agrona - Goddess of battle slaughter.

Alator - A god of war depicted with helmet, shield, and spear.

Albiorix - Another god of war with a name derived from the ancient term for Britain - Albu or Alba (to the Romans: Albion).

Andrasta - Little is known about this goddess. Queen Boudica (?–AD 61) of the Celtic Iceni tribe, is supposed to have called upon her when she led a rebellion against the Romans.

Antenociticus (alternately, Anociticus or Antocidicus) - A young god whose one statue displayed hair frozen in the style of a young stag's antlers. His three known altars were discovered near Hadrian's Wall in the north of England.

Arecurius - God of northeast England during Roman occupation. His name signifies, "he who stands before the tribe."

Arnemetia (alternately, Arnomecte) - Goddess with inscriptions found at two locations in Derbyshire, England - a sacred spring close to Buxton and altar at Brough-on-Noe, in a Roman fort built there.

Barrex (alternately, Barrecis) - Another god of war, associated with Roman Mars. Inscription found in Carlisle, northern England.

Belatucadrus - Another god of war, associated with Roman Mars, worshipped in northern England. By the large number of variations in spelling, scholars suspect that this god was particularly important to the Celtic lower class, who held poorer skills in literacy.

Boand (alternately, Boann, Boin, or Boinne) - Goddess of eastern Ireland's Boyne River.

Bodb (alternately Badb or Bave) - The name of two mythological figures: 1) Son of the Dagda in the Irish Mythological Cycle, and 2) A female demon who appears on battlefields in the form of a crow.

Braciaca - A minor war god mentioned only once in central England. Romans compared him to Mars.

Canomagus - God of hounds. A votive inscription found in southwestern England at Nettleton Shrub mentioned this god and the Greco-Roman god, Apollo.

Cocidius - A hunting or war god shown with a dog, a stag, wearing hooded cloak, and holding shield and spear. Worshippers included Roman soldiers. Inscriptions associate him with Roman gods Mars (war) and Silvanus (woods) and an otherwise unknown Celtic god named Vernostonus.

Contrebus - A minor god mentioned in northwest England. Meaning: "he who lives among us."

Corotiacus - Another minor war god associated with Roman Mars. Mentioned at Martlesham, Suffolk, England.

Coventina - A goddess in the form of a water nymph, also depicted as three nymphs. Her one sanctuary was located near Hadrian's Wall in northern England.

The Dagda - The chief god of the Irish and leader of the group of good gods called "Tuatha Dé Dannan." In fact, his name is thought to mean "the good god."

Daron - A minor goddess identified with oak trees.

Deva - A minor British goddess. Locals gave her name to the River Dee found in southwest England and northern Wales.

Eochaid - A god of the Sun, horses, and lightning.

Ernmas - Goddess and mother of the three war goddesses mentioned in the Irish Mythological Cycle - Bodb, Macha, and the Mórrigan. Her name derives from Celtic words which convey the meaning, "death from weapons."

Lenus - A war god associated with Roman Mars. Inscriptions mentioning him were found in Chedworth (southwestern England) and Caerwent (southern Wales).

Macha - A war goddess (or demon) who is sister of Bodb and the Mórrigan. A daughter of the Dagda.

Matunus - A minor god of northern England with a name referring to the animal bear (genus *Ursus*).

Medb (alternately Maeve) - Goddess of sovereignty who, in the Ulster Cycle, was the wife of Ailill, king of Connacht.

Medocius - Another war god worshipped in southeastern England, near Colchester.

The Mórrigan - War goddess (or demon) and a key figure in Irish mythology, and frequently associated with her sisters, Bodb and Macha.

Nehalennia - A minor goddess frequently shown holding a fruit basket, wearing a short cape and seated next to a dog. Worshipped in northeastern England and in the Netherlands.

Neít - Another war god of Ireland. He is the husband of Nemain.

Nemain - Goddess of confusion on the battlefield. Her husband is Neít.

Nodons (alternately Nodens or Nudens) - A god of healing and patron of dogs. Romans compared him to Mars. Some scholars suggest that his name means "fisherman-hunter." Evidence of his worship was found in northwestern and southwestern England.

Ocelus - Another war god worshipped in northwestern England, southern Wales, and perhaps between the two regions.

Sulis - Goddess of healing. Romans compared her to Minerva. Aquae Sulis, a healing spring in Bath, England, was named after her.

Verbeia - A goddess worshipped in northeastern England at the old Roman fort named Ilkley. Her image is shown grasping a snake in each hand.

Vernostonus - A minor god worshipped in northern England. Evidence suggests that Roman soldiers look upon him with favor.

Veteris (alternately, Vitiris or Vitris) - A god worshipped in northern England.

France (Gaul)

Ahes - A goddess and patroness of roads, recognized as the reason for constructing the Roman roads found throughout Brittany.

Alisonus (alternately, Alisanos) - A god linked to rocky outcroppings or to the rocks themselves. Possibly related to the Alisos River. Worshipped in central eastern France.

Amarcolitanus - A god whose name seems to mean "he of the distant gaze." Romans compared him to Apollo. Worshipped in eastern France.

Andarta - A goddess of the bear (taxonomic family *Ursus*), worshipped in southern France, near Die.

Artaius - A god named after bears. Romans compared him to Mercury, the messenger god. Worshipped in southeastern France, near Beaucroissant.

Atepomarus - A god worshipped in central France, near Mauvières. Romans compared him to Apollo.

Atesmerius - A god (or goddess?) worshipped in northeastern France, in the lower Marne region. He was an important deity of the Meldi tribe. Evidence survives at what was the Meldi capital, Meaux, with another inscription found in western France at Poitiers. The latter inscription spells the name "Adsmerius." In the Marne region's Corgebin forest, an inscription was found paying tribute to a goddess named Atesmerta. Was this the same deity with an alternate spelling, or was it a different entity?

Belisama (alternately, Belesama or Belisma) - A goddess of rivers and lakes. Her name means "the most shining" or "bright one." While we have evidence of her worship in southern France, near Orange, place names throughout France find her as their origin.

Bergusia - A goddess worshipped in eastern Gaul, near Alesia, where stood the primary settlement of the Mandubii tribe. Consort of the god known as Ucuetis, she may also be patroness of crafts.

Bodua - A war goddess of Gaul.

Bolvinnus - Another war god, worshipped in central France, near Bouhy.

Bormana - A goddess and occasional consort of the god, Borvo.

Borvo (also Bormo) - A god associated with natural hot springs and whose name seems to mean "to boil." Two natural springs are named after him: Bourbonne-les-Bains (eastern France) and Bourbon-Lancy (central France). If we account for alternate spellings, this god may also be known farther afield with names like Bormana, Bormanus, and in Portugal, Bormanicus. Several inscriptions to him mention a consort named Bormana or Damona.

Britovius - A war god worshipped in southern France, near Nîmes. And naturally, the Romans compared him to Mars.

Budenicus - Yet another war god worshipped in southern France, near Uzès. Romans compared him to Mars, their god of war.

Buxenus - Another war god worshipped in southeastern France, near Velleron. Romans compared him to Mars.

Cathubodua - A war goddess worshipped in eastern France, near Haute-Savoie.

Cicolluis - A god of protection who was worshipped in central eastern France at places like Aignay-le-Duc, Mâlain, and Dijon, and in northern Switzerland at Windisch. His name, based on Celtic root words, seems to be "Great Protector," thus the Romans compared him to their god of war, Mars. His name is frequently given with that of his consort, the goddess Litavis.

Cososus - A Celtic war god worshipped in central France, at Bourges, and compared by the Romans to Mars.

Damona - A goddess whose name seems to be based on the Celtic root word for "cow." A number of inscriptions found in Gaul name her as the god Borvo's consort. An inscription found in northeastern France names her as the god Albius's consort. And the remnants of a statue found in Alesia name her as consort of the god Moritasgus.

Dinomogetimarus - A war god worshipped in southern France, at Saint-Pons. The single inscription names him along with the god Divanno, both of whom the Romans compared to Mars.

Divanno - A war god worshipped in southern France, at Saint-Pons. The single inscription names him along with the god Dinomogetimarus, both of whom the Romans compared to Mars.

Dumiatis - A war god worshipped in central France, near Clermont-Ferrand. Evidence of his cult came in the form of a bronze plaque found at a Roman-Gallic hilltop temple. Romans compared him to Mars.

Erriapus - A god worshipped in the Garonne region of southern Gaul.

Esus - A god worshipped across Gaul. One monument pictures him as a man with a beard standing next to a tree, holding a sickle for trimming branches. Pictured nearby are three cranes and a bull. Some Roman authors commented how human sacrifices were made in his name.

Glanis - God of a healing spring with a shrine to his honor in southern Gaul, at Glanum. Scholars suspect that he is a key member of a trio of gods known as Glanicae.

Icuana - Goddess of the Yonne River, which flows into the River Seine, in central northern France.

Leherennus - A war god of southwestern France, near Ardiège, thought by some scholars to be pre-Celtic. Romans compare him to Mars.

Litavis - A war goddess worshipped in northeastern France and consort of Cicollus. Her name is thought to mean "broad" or "earth." Romans compare her to Mars.

Luxovius - Water god worshipped in eastern France, near Luxeuil, the location of a natural spring. Brixia is his consort.

Matrona (frequently Dea Matrona) - A mother goddess worshipped in northeastern Gaul. She has been linked to the Marne River. [see also Matronae (Main Deities)]

Moccus - A god worshipped in northeastern France, near Langres. His name has a linguistic affinity to the word "pig" in Celtic. Though the Romans compared him to Mercury, he is thought to have been a protector of boar hunters.

Mogetius - A god worshipped in central France, near Bourges, and in Austria, near Seggau. Romans compared him to Mars.

Moltinus - A god of sheep or rams, worshipped in eastern France, near Mâcon. The god was also mentioned in Austria, near Innsbruck, in a curse tablet.

Moritasgus - A god worshipped in eastern France, near Alesia. One damaged statue identifies Damona as his consort. Romans compared him to Apollo.

Mullo - A god of hills or mules worshipped in northwestern Gaul, near Allones, Craon, Nantes, and Rennes. Some scholars suspect him to have also been a healing god, specifically for the eyes.

Nabelcus - A war god worshipped in southeastern France, near Saint-Didier. Romans compared him to Mars.

Nantosuelta - A goddess worshipped throughout much of Gaul. There are several mentions of her as the god Sucellus's consort. Images of the goddess show her holding a scepter with a tiny house on top.

Rosmerta - A goddess of motherhood and fertility worshipped in northeastern Gaul. She was frequently associated with Mercury and even shown holding his staff - the caduceus.

Rudianus - A god of war worshipped in southwestern France. And, of course, Romans compared him to Mars.

Rudiobus - A god worshipped in central France, near Neuvy-en-Sullias. The only mention of him was found at the foot of a horse statue.

Segomo - A horse god worshipped in eastern central Gaul, especially by the Sequani tribe. Romans compared him to Mars.

Sequana - A goddess of healing. The River Seine goes by her name in the Celtic language. The Celts had placed a sanctuary to her near Dijon, at the source of the river.

Smertius (alternately Smertrios) - A god of providence and protection. On a votive column found underneath Notre-Dame in Paris, the god's name is mentioned with an image of him wearing a beard, holding club in one hand and the tail of a snake in the other, with the clear intent to strike the reptile.

Souconna - A goddess worshipped in eastern France, associated with the River Saône.

Sutugius - A war god worshipped in southwestern France, near Saint-Placard. Some scholars suspect he has a pre-Celtic origin.

Tarvos Trigaranus - A god whose name has had limited mention, but who may have had a far broader influence. The name means "bull with three cranes," and this symbolism has been found in numerous places throughout Europe, including on the first century AD monument founder under the Paris Notre-Dame cathedral, named the Nautae Parisiaci, and including a stele discovered in western Germany, near Trier. The enigmatic myth behind these symbols remains unknown, but it may be related to the god Esus.

Ucuetis - God of industry and patron of craftworkers, worshipped in northeastern France, near Alesia. Images of him show him holding a hammer. One inscription mentioned that his consort is the goddess Bergusia.

Vindonnus - A god thought to be related to curing eye ailments, worshipped in northeastern France, near Essarois. Romans compared him to their healing god, Apollo.

Visucius - A god worshipped in northeastern France, near Bordeaux, and in Belgium, the Netherlands, and Luxembourg. Romans compared him to Mercury.

Vorocius - A god worshipped in central France, near Vichy. Romans compared him to Mars.

Vosegus - A god worshipped in eastern France. His name was given to a forest in that region, home to the Vogesen tribe. Images of the god show him holding pinecones and nuts, and carrying a piglet.

Iberia

Very little documentation could be found for the Celtic gods and goddesses of Iberia, but here is a list of some of the known deities of Celtic Spain and Portugal:

Aernus [M], Aetio [M], Araco [M], Ares Lusitani [M], Asidiae [F], Ataegina (alternately, Ataecina) [F], Bandua [M], Besenclā (alternately Besenclae) [F], Bormanicus (alternately, Bormo or Borvo) [M], Broeneiae [F], Cariocecus [M], Carneo [M], Cohue [M], Coruae [F], Cosuneae [F], Cosus (alternately Coso or Cossue) [M], Crouga [M], Crougeae (alternately Corougiae) [F], Deae sanctae (alternately Burrulobrigensi) [F], Deiba [F], Deo Nemedeco [M], Deo Paramaeco [M], Duberdicus [M], Endovelicus [M], Epane (alternately, Epona or Iccona) [F], Erbina [F], Ermae [F], Erriapus [M], Flauiae Conimbriga (alternately, Flauiae Conimbrigae) [F], Ilurbeda [F], Issibaeo [M], Kuanikio (alternately, Quangeio or Quangeius) [M], Lacipaea (alternately, Lacibiā or Lacibea) [F], Laneana (alternately, Laneanis) [F], Losa [F], Lugus [M], Luna Augusta [F], Mermandiceo [M], Mirobleo [F], Munidis [F], Nabia (alternately, Navia) [F], Nymphis [F], Ocrimirae [F], Picio [M], Reo [M], Reva (alternately Reua) [F], Salama [M], Sucellus [M], Tabaliaenus [M], Tabudico [M], Toga [F], Tongoenabiagus [M], Trebaruna [F], Trebopala [F], Turiacus [M], Tutelae [F], Visucius [M], Vorteaeceo [M].

Germany and Eastern Europe

Abnoba - A hunting goddess worshipped in southeast Germany's Black Forest region. A figurine made of sandstone, found in Karlsruhe-Mühlburg, shows her with a hunting dog holding a wild hare. Romans compared her to their hunting goddess, Diana.

Arduinna - A goddess associated with boars and mountains, and worshipped in the forests of the Rhine River. Romans compared her to goddess Diana.

Artio - A goddess of the bear (taxonomic family *Ursus*). Evidence of her worship has been found in western Germany, near Trier, and at Muri, near Berne, Switzerland. One image of her shows her seated and offering to a bear a bowl of fruit.

Arvernorix - A god worshipped in southern Germany, near Miltenberg in Bavaria. However, his name means, "King of the Averni," a Celtic tribe found in central France, in the Auvergne region.

Arvernus (variation of Arvernorix?) - A god worshipped along the banks of the Rhine River in Germany. Romans compared him to the god Mercury.

Caturix - A war god worshipped in southern Germany, near Böckingen, and throughout Switzerland. His name means "king of battle." Romans compared him to their god of war, Mars.

Cnabetius - A god worshipped in western Germany, near Hüttigweiler, Tholey, and Wahlscheid, and in southern Germany, near Osteburken.

Gebrinius - A god who some scholars suspect may be of Germanic origin. Inscriptions with his name have been found under a cathedral in Bonn, Germany. Romans compared him to their god Mercury.

Intarabus - A war god worshipped in Belgium, near Foy, and in western Germany, near Trier. Romans compared him to Mars.

Iovantucarus - A god worshipped in western Germany, at Heidenburg, Tholey, and Trier. Romans have compared him at various times to the god Mars and to the god Mercury.

Latobius - A minor god worshipped in Austria, near Noricum.

Noreia - A goddess worshipped in northern Slovenia and southern Austria.

Sirona (alternately, Dirona) - A goddess worshipped across Germany, Austria, and France, usually at natural springs. Her name means "star." In images she is shown wearing a long robe, while she holds wheat, eggs, or grapes. By this, scholars suspect she is a fertility goddess. Throughout the Roman Celtic culture, she is a common consort of the Roman god Apollo. She has also been known as the companion of the Celtic god Grannus.

Toutiorix - A god worshipped in eastern Germany, near Wiesbaden. His name means "king of the tribal group." Romans compared him to their god Apollo.

Archaeological Links to Celtic Mythology

Archaeologists have been able to systematically examine the physical remains of the ancient Celts, both their bodies and also the remnants of their homes, camps and tools, which offers a look at the day-to-day lives of the people. Mythology and belief, which are fundamentally intangible, are far less conducive to archaeological research, but archaeology still helps. For example, by examining the scant written record from Roman observers, it's known that the most famous order of Celtic priests, the Druids, neither kept written records nor built physical temples, instead preferring to worship in open groves[25]. Furthermore, one infamous survival of Celtic ritual and myth is the "bog men," the victims of ritualized homicide in swamps throughout Britain and Ireland. There is still debate as to whether these individuals were killed as punishment for crime or as a part of a religious offering, but a growing amount of evidence in the archaeological remains support the ancient Roman texts that claimed human sacrifice was regularly demanded by Celtic gods[26]. An example is the "Lindow Man," a body found in a swamp in northwestern England. From roughly the late Celtic or early Roman period, he was strangled, his throat was cut, and his head was hit. This combination, along with his well-fed and groomed body, indicate a ritual event.[27]

---

25 *The Druids: The History and Mystery of the Ancient Celtic Priests* by Jesse Harasta (2013). Charles Rivers Editors.
26 "Druids committed Human Sacrifice, Cannibalism?" accessed online at:
http://news.nationalgeographic.com/news/2009/03/090320-druids-sacrifice-cannibalism.html
27 Lindow Man/Lindow II" at the British Museum homepage, accessed online at:
http://www.britishmuseum.org/research/collection_online/collection_object_details.aspx?objectId=808672&partId=1

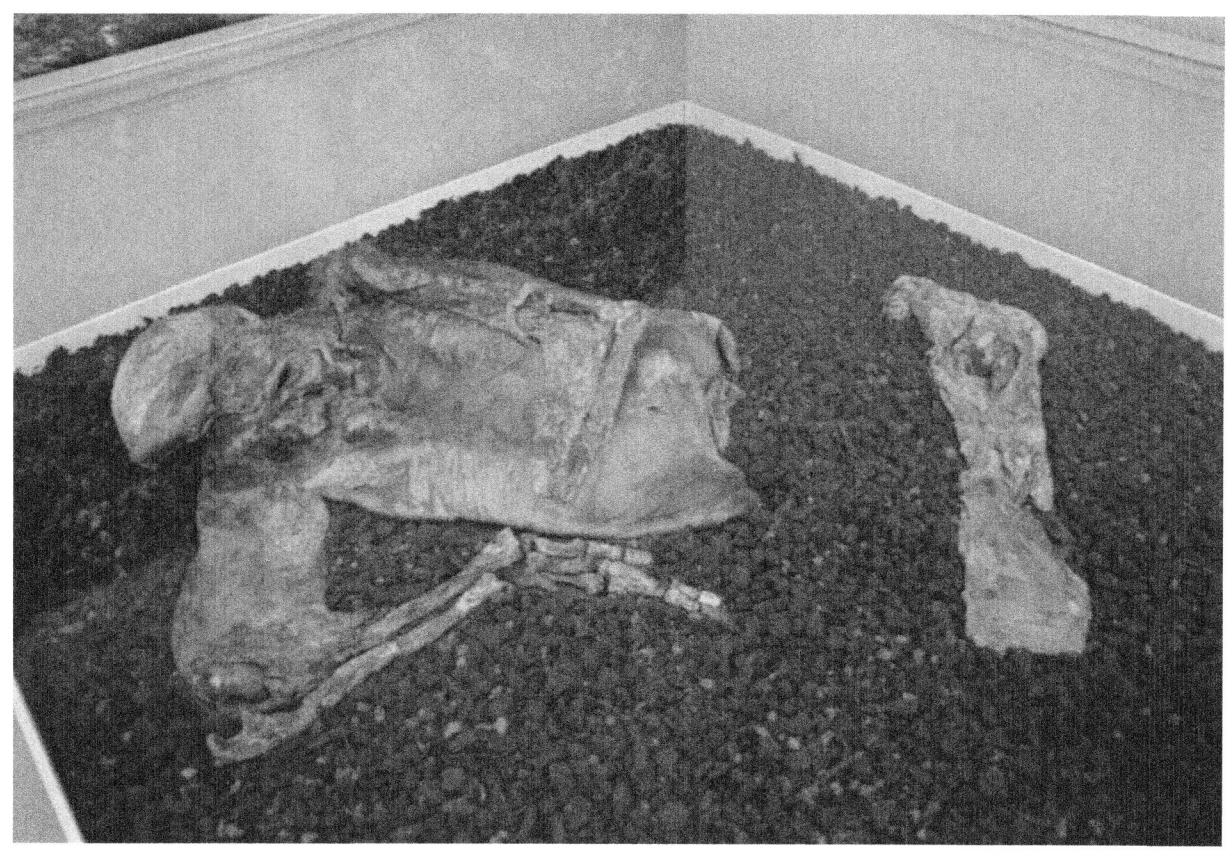

The remains of Lindow Man. Picture taken by Mike Peel.

In addition to the bodies, another physical remnant of Celtic mythology from the pre-Roman period are the Celts' beautiful works of art, many of which are held in the British Museum and some of which have been associated with religious beliefs. One common class of item are decorated bronze spoons, often perforated with holes, which have been found in bogs associated with ritual deaths[28]. Another example is a piece in the British Museum: an iron headband dating to 200-150 BC, decorated in elaborate swirling patterns. Its current interpretation is that it was worn by a priest (perhaps a Druid), and its association with weapons in the tomb shows that the priestly order may have been military in nature (an association that is also made in Roman texts describing battles between Druids)[29]. That said, it is probable that the swirling patterns themselves, so typical of Celtic work and still popular in Celtic influenced art today, had a symbolic meaning, perhaps showing a cyclical nature of the universe or even representing the faith in the way that the Cross does for Christianity. They also depict numerous images of animals, often in a stylized, spindly form.

---

28 "The Druids" at the British Museum homepage, accessed online at:
   http://www.britishmuseum.org/explore/highlights/articles/d/the_druids.aspx
29 "Skull and Crown of the 'Deal Warrior'" at the British Museum homepage, accessed online at:
   http://www.britishmuseum.org/explore/highlights/highlight_objects/pe_prb/s/skull__crown_of_deal_warrior.aspx

The Druids

The Celts have fascinated people for centuries, and the biggest fascination of all has been over the Druids, a religious class at the heart of Celtic society that wielded great power. Naturally, people have been interested in Druids for centuries mostly because they don't understand much about the Druids or their practices. There is even considerable debate about the etymology of the word "Druid." The first steps of this word are relatively clear: "Druid" in English comes from "Druide" in French (perhaps in the 1560s), and this comes from the Latin "Druidae", which was the term used by the ancient Roman chroniclers in reference to the white robed order of Celtic priests living in Gaul, Britain and Ireland. However, the more interesting and useful question is what is the origin of the term in Latin. Did the chroniclers invent the word, or was it borrowed from some Gaulish or other Celtic terminology? If the latter is true, then understanding the origins of "Druidae" may explain how the ancient Celts saw their religious leaders, much the same way insights can be gained from analyzing the Christian title "pastor," which is drawn from the term for someone who cares for a flock of animals and says something about the ways that early Christians viewed their spiritual leaders.

Unfortunately, the modern Celtic languages do not provide much help, because their terms for Druids are typically borrowed from English, as with the Cornish word "drewyth ("drewydhyon" for the plural).[30] However, for over a century, scholars have examined the extant Celtic tongues and compared them to the written fragments of earlier incarnations to attempt to reconstruct a language they call Old Celtic, and by examining the hypothetical words of Old Celtic (for which there are no written records), scholars can propose theories of the origins of words like "Druidae." One of the most convincing of these arguments is that the word was "Druides" in Gaulish, which was the language of the Celts who fought against the Roman chroniclers, and that it in turn came from a hypothetical Old Celtic word "*derwijes[31]." This would have come from "*dru" (which meant "tree" or "oak") and "*wid-" (which meant "to know" or "to have a vision"). This would mean that the roots would be something akin to "those who know the oak." Interestingly, the Old Celtic word "*derwos" also meant "truth," a double meaning that was probably not lost on the Celts[32].

There is one other potential origin of the term worth noting. The Celtic languages are divided into two large groups: the Brythonic (including today's Welsh, Breton and Cornish and historical Gaulish and British) and Goedelic (including today's Irish, Scot's Gaelic and Manx and the historic languages of Ireland). The term "*derwijes" is derived from the Brythonic side of the language family, which makes sense considering that the Romans primarily encountered

---

30 In Nance's classic 1952 *A New Cornish Dictionary* (pg 43), the term is further attributed from borrowing from Welsh and Breton.
31 In historical linguistics, words which have been reconstructed in the manner I described, but have no concrete records in the written word are marked with a "*" to denote them as hypothetical.
32 "Druid" in the *Oxford English Online Etymology Dictionary* accessed online at: http://www.etymonline.com/index.php?term=Druid

speakers of Brythonic languages in Gaul and Britain. However, in the contemporary Irish and Scots languages, the term "draoi" comes from "druadh", which means a "magician" or "sorcerer." This comes from an Old Irish term "drui" with the same meaning. What gives this argument some plausibility that the first one does not have is that the words "draoi," "druadh" and "drui" can all be found in either modern spoken language or in written records, not merely through hypothetical reconstruction.

Given that the primary sources of information about druids come from the writings of the Roman enemies, historians take them with a grain of salt because the Romans were hardly an unbiased source. Nonetheless, some ancient writers went into exacting detail about Celtic society and the Celts' infamous religious class. Even before the rise of the Roman Empire, ancient historians described the Celts and some of their rituals. According to the ancient Greek historian Athenaeus, in the 4th century B.C., Sopater noted, "Among them is the custom, whenever they are victorious in battle, to sacrifice their prisoners to the gods. So I, like the Celts, have vowed to the divine powers to burn those three false dialecticians as an offering." In the early 3rd century B.C., Timaeus wrote, "Historians point out that the Celts who live on the shore of the Ocean honor the Dioscori above other gods. For there is an ancient tradition among them that these gods came to them from the Ocean."

Another Greek historian noted their use of sacrifices: "Eudoxus says that the Celts do the following (and if anyone thinks his account credible, let him believe it; if not, let him ignore it). When clouds of locusts invade their country and damage the crops, the Celts evoke certain prayers and offer sacrifices which charm birds - and the birds hear these prayers, come in flocks, and destroy the locusts. If however one of them should capture one of these birds, his punishment according to the laws of the country is death. If he is pardoned and released, this throws the birds into a rage, and to revenge the captured bird they do not respond if they are called on again." Strabo noted a similar anecdote: "The following story which Artemidorus has told about the crows is unbelievable. There is a certain harbor on the coast which, according to him, is named 'Two Crows'. In this harbor are seen two crows, with their right wings somewhat white. Men who are in dispute about certain matters come here, put a plank on an elevated place, and then each man separately throws up cakes of barley. The birds fly up and eat some of the cakes, but scatter others. The man whose cakes are scattered wins the dispute. Although this story is implausible, his report about the goddesses Demeter and Core is more credible. He says that there is an island near Britain on which sacrifices are performed like those in Samothrace for Demeter and Core."

Ultimately, the most concrete descriptions of the Druids came from several Roman writers, who offer tantalizing glimpses into the lost religious and ritual world of the Druids and overwhelmingly demonstrate the social power that the Druids had and the ways that Romans seemed to often hold them in awe as well. For example, the Roman writer Diodorus Siculus, who lived during the mid-1st century B.C., described the inhabitants of Gaul in detail, and the

Romans knew them all too well as a result of Julius Caesar's campaigns in Gaul. Diodorus wrote:

""The Gauls have certain wise men and experts on the gods called Druids, as well as a highly respected class of seers. Through auguries and animal sacrifice these seers predict the future and no one dares to scoff at them. They have an especially odd and unbelievable method of divination for the most important matters. Having anointed a human victim, they stab him with a small knife in the area above the diaphragm. When the man has collapsed from the wound, they interpret the future by observing the nature of his fall, the convulsion of his limbs, and especially from the pattern of his spurting blood. In this type of divination, the seers place great trust in an ancient tradition of observation.

It is a custom among the Gauls to never perform a sacrifice without someone skilled in divine ways present. They say that those who know about the nature of the gods should offer thanks to them and make requests of them, as though these people spoke the same language as the gods. The Gauls, friends and foes alike, obey the rule of the priests and bards not only in time of peace but also during wars. It has often happened that just as two armies approached each other with swords drawn and spears ready, the Druids will step between the two sides and stop the fighting, as if they had cast a spell on wild beasts. Thus even among the wildest barbarians, anger yields to wisdom and the god of war respects the Muses…

It is in keeping with their wildness and savage nature that they carry out particularly offensive religious practices. They will keep some criminal under guard for five years, then impale him on a pole in honor of their gods - followed by burning him on an enormous pyre along with many other first-fruits. They also use prisoners of war as sacrifices to the gods. Some of the Gauls will even sacrifice animals captured in war, either by slaying them, burning them, or by killing them with some other type of torture."

Perhaps the most detailed discussion of the Druids and their ways comes from Julius Caesar's *Notebooks About the Gallic War*, written some time in the 50s or 40s BC. He discusses Celtic society and the Druids at length:

"Throughout Gaul there are two classes of persons of definite account and dignity…Of the two classes above mentioned one consists of Druids, the other of knights. The former are concerned with divine worship, the due performance of sacrifices, public and private, and the interpretation of ritual questions: a great number of young men gather about them for the sake of instruction and hold them in great honour.

A great many young men come to the Druids for instruction, holding them in great respect. Indeed, the Druids are the judges on all controversies public and private. If any crime has been committed, if any murder done, if there are any questions concerning inheritance, or any controversy concerning boundaries, the Druids decide the case and determine punishments. If anyone ignores their decision, that person is banned from all sacrifices - an extremely harsh punishment among the Gauls. Those who are so condemned are considered detestable criminals. Everyone shuns them and will not speak with them, fearing some harm from contact with them, and they receive no justice nor honor for any worthy deed.

Among all the Druids there is one who is the supreme leader, holding highest authority over the rest. When the chief Druid dies, whoever is the most worthy succeeds him. If there are several of equal standing, a vote of all the Druids follows, though the leadership is sometimes contested even by armed force. At a certain time of the year, all the Druids gather together at a consecrated spot in the territory of the Carnutes, whose land is held to be the center of all Gaul. Everyone gathers therefrom the whole land to present disputes and they obey the judgments and decrees of the Druids. It is said that the Druidic movement began in Britain and was then carried across to Gaul. Even today, those who wish to study their teachings most diligently usually travel to Britain.

The Druids are exempt from serving in combat and from paying war taxes, unlike all other Gauls. Tempted by such advantages, many young people willingly commit themselves to Druidic studies while others are sent by their parents. It is said that in the schools of the Druids they learn a great number of verses, so many in fact that some students spend twenty years in training. It is not permitted to write down any of these sacred teachings, though other public and private transactions are often recorded in Greek letters. I believe they practice this oral tradition for two reasons: first, so that the common crowd does not gain access to their secrets and second, to improve the faculty of memory. Truly, writing does often weaken one's diligence in learning and reduces the ability to memorize. The cardinal teaching of the Druids is that the soul does not perish, but after death passes from one body to another. Because of this teaching that death is only a transition, they are able to encourage fearlessness in battle. They have a great many other teachings as well which they hand down to the young concerning such things as the motion of the stars, the size of the cosmos and the earth, the order of the natural world, and the power of the immortal gods.

All of the Gauls are greatly devoted to religion, and because of this those who are afflicted with terrible illnesses or face dangers in battle will conduct human sacrifices, or at least vow to do so. The Druids are the ministers at such occasions. They believe that unless the life of a person is offered for the life of another, the dignity of the immortal gods will be insulted. This is true both in private and public sacrifices. Some build enormous figures which they fill with living persons and then set on fire, everyone perishing inflames. They believe that the execution of thieves and other criminals is the most pleasing to the gods, but, when the supply of guilty persons runs short, they will kill the innocent as well.

The chief god of the Gauls is Mercury and there are images of him everywhere. He is said to be the inventor of all the arts, the guide for every road and journey, and the most influential god in trade and moneymaking. After him, they worship Apollo, Mars, Jupiter, and Minerva. These gods have the same areas of influence as among most other peoples. Apollo drives away diseases, Minerva is most influential in crafts, Jupiter rules the sky, and Mars is the god of war. Before a great battle, they will often dedicate the spoils to Mars. If they are successful, they will sacrifice all the living things they have captured and other spoils they gather together in one place. Among many tribes, you can see these spoils placed together in a sacred spot. And it is a very rare occasion that anyone would dare to disturb these valuable goods and conceal them in his home. If it does happen, the perpetrator is tortured and punished in the worst ways imaginable.

The Gauls all say that they are descended from the god of the dark underworld, Dis, and confirm that this is the teaching of the Druids. Because of this they measure time by the passing of nights, not days. Birthdays and the beginnings of months and years all start at night.

The funerals of the Gauls are magnificent and extravagant. Everything which was dear to the departed is thrown into the fire, including animals. In the recent past, they would also burn faithful slaves and beloved subordinates at the climax of the funeral."[33]

Caesar, while writing something of a puff-piece in *Notebooks*, certainly had firsthand knowledge of the Druids from his time fighting the Gauls and was thus an invaluable direct observer. While probably writing from second-hand sources, Strabo gave a similar description of the Druids' high status in his seminal *Geography*, which was published in the first decade of the 1st century B.C., before Caesar's work: "Among all the Gallic peoples, generally speaking, there are three sets of men who are held in exceptional honour; the Bards, the Vates and the Druids. The Bards are singers and poets; the Vates, diviners and natural philosophers; while the Druids, in addition to natural philosophy, study also moral philosophy."[34] Caesar's observation that the Druids acted like judges for social disputes was also echoed by Strabo, who wrote, "The Druids are considered the most just of men, and on this account they are entrusted with the decision, not only of the private disputes, but of the public disputes as well; so that, in former times, they even arbitrated cases of war and made the opponents stop when they were about to line up for battle, and the murder cases, in particular, had been turned over to them for decision. Further, when there is a big yield from these cases, there is forthcoming a big yield from the land too, as they think." Strabo also seems to confirm Caesar's description of the Druids' religious beliefs about the immortality of the soul: "However, not only the Druids, but others as well, say that men's souls, and also the universe, are indestructible, although both fire and water will at some time or other prevail over them."

---

33 All of the Caesar quotes are from: *The Gallic War* by Julius Caesar, Book VI Chapters 13-14. Accessed online at: http://penelope.uchicago.edu/Thayer/E/Roman/Texts/Caesar/Gallic_War/6B*.html#13
34 All of the Strabo quotes come from *The Geography Book IV, Chapter 4:4* accessed online at: http://penelope.uchicago.edu/Thayer/E/Roman/Texts/Strabo/4D*.html#4.4

While these theological points may have been of some interest to the Romans, one area of religious practice that always intrigued ancient writers was divination: the ability to tell the future or of far off events. The famous Roman orator and philosopher Cicero described the Druids, amongst the religious practitioners of several foreign peoples, in his work *De Divinatione* (*"Of Divination"*). He wrote, "Nor is the practice of divination disregarded even among uncivilized tribes, if indeed there are Druids in Gaul - and there are, for I knew one of them myself, Divitiacus, the Aeduan, your guest and eulogist. He claimed to have that knowledge of nature which the Greeks call 'physiologia,' and he used to make predictions, sometimes by means of augury and sometimes by means of conjecture."[35] Strabo also mentioned Druidic divination: "They used to strike a human being, whom they had devoted to death, in the back with a sabre, and then divine from his death-struggle. But they would not sacrifice without the Druids."[36]

Pliny also noted the Celts' use of divination and human sacrifice in the 1st century A.D.:

"I can't forget to mention the admiration the Gauls have for mistletoe. The Druids (which is the name of their holy men) hold nothing more sacred than this plant and the tree on which it grows - as if it grew only on oaks. They worship only in oak groves and will perform no sacred rites unless a branch of that tree is present. It seems the Druids even get their name from drus (the Greek word for oak). And indeed they think that anything which grows on an oak tree is sent from above and is a sign that the tree was selected by the god himself. The problem is that in fact mistletoe rarely grows on oak trees. Still they search it out with great diligence and then will cut it only on the sixth day of the moon's cycle, because the moon is then growing in power but is not yet halfway through its course (they use the moon to measure not only months but years and their grand cycle of thirty years). In their language they call mistletoe a name meaning "all-healing". They hold sacrifices and sacred meals under oak trees, first leading forward two white bulls with horns bound for the first time. A priest dressed in white then climbs the tree and cuts the mistletoe with a golden sickle, with the plant dropping onto a white cloak. They then sacrifice the bulls while praying that the god will favorably grant his own gift to those to whom he has given it. They believe a drink made with mistletoe will restore fertility to barren livestock and act as a remedy to all poisons. Such is the devotion to frivolous affairs shown by many peoples.

Similar to the Sabine herb savin is a plant called selago. It must be picked without an iron instrument by passing the right hand through the opening of the left sleeve, as if you were stealing it. The harvester, having first offered bread and wine, must wear white and have clean, bare feet. It is carried in a new piece of cloth. The Druids of Gaul say that it is should be used to ward off every danger and that the smoke of burning selago is good for eye diseases. The

---

35 *De Divinatione* Book I 41:90, accessed online at:
  http://penelope.uchicago.edu/Thayer/E/Roman/Texts/Cicero/de_Divinatione/1*.html
36 Strabo's *The Geography Book IV, Chapter 4:5*

Druids also gather a plant from marshes called samolus, which must be picked with the left hand during a time of fasting. It is good for the diseases of cows, but the one who gathers it must not look back nor place it anywhere except in the watering trough of the animals.

There is a kind of egg which is very famous in Gaul but ignored by Greek writers. In the summer months, a vast number of snakes will gather themselves together in a ball which is held together by their saliva and a secretion from their bodies. The Druids say they produce this egg-like object called an anguinum which the hissing snakes throw up into the air. It must be caught, so they say, in a cloak before it hits the ground. But you'd better have a horse handy, because the snakes will chase you until they are cut off by some stream. A genuine anguinum will float upstream, even if covered in gold. But as is common with the world's holy men, the Druids say it can only be gathered during a particular phase of the moon, as if people could make the moon and serpents work together. I saw one of these eggs myself - it was a small round thing like an apple with a hard surface full of indentations as on the arms of an octopus. The Druids value them highly. They say it is a great help in lawsuits and will help you gain the good will of a ruler. That this is plainly false is shown by a man of the Gaulish Vocontii tribe, a Roman knight, who kept one hidden in his cloak during a trial before the emperor Claudius and was executed, as far as I can tell, for this reason alone.

Barbarous rites were found in Gaul even within my own memory. For it was then that the emperor Tiberius passed a decree through the senate outlawing their Druids and these types of diviners and physicians. But why do I mention this about a practice which has crossed the sea and reached the ends of the earth? For even today Britain performs rites with such ceremony that you would think they were the source for the extravagant Persians. It is amazing how distant people are so similar in such practices. But at least we can be glad that the Romans have wiped out the murderous cult of the Druids, who thought human sacrifice and ritual cannibalism were the greatest kind of piety."[37]

In this excerpt, Pliny offers perhaps the richest detail of all of the ancient sources. His account includes details of Druidic ritual - the use of oak groves, the importance of mistletoe - that were not noted anywhere else, and it's perhaps no coincidence that worship in oaken groves was not unique to the Druids, as there is evidence that the Germanic god Thor/Donar was worshiped primarily in this context as well.[38]

Perhaps most importantly, Pliny provides an evocative image that has influenced all later images of the Druids: a white-robed priest with a golden sickle climbing an oak tree to harvest mistletoe while two white bulls bellow on the floor of the grove below.[39] He also notes that the

---

37 *Natural History* by Pliny the Elder, Volume 3, Book XVI: Chapter 95
38 *Thor: The Origins, History and Evolution of the Norse God* by Jesse Harasta (2013). Charles River Editors.
39 A sickle is a hand tool with a handle and a curved blade perhaps as long as a forearm. It was used for harvesting grain and hay.

Druids used a lunar calendar that began their months on the fifth day of the lunar cycle and was divided up into months, years and 'ages[40].' The Romans, on the other hand, used a solar calendar that they dated back to the founding of their city ("the Calendar of Romulus"), and a revised form of that calendar is still used across the West today. The existence of a calendar is itself a tribute to the Druids' learning and their ability to not only carefully track celestial motions but also perform relatively complex mathematics; the fact that they apparently did so without writing is even more impressive (though not unique, as the civilizations of the Andes also created elaborate calendars without writing).[41]

The famous Roman historian Livy wrote of a grisly anecdote in the 1st century A.D. about Celtic sacrifice: "Postumius died there fighting with all his might not to be captured alive. The Gauls stripped him of all his spoils and the Boii took his severed head in a procession to the holiest of their temples. There it was cleaned and the bare skull was adorned with gold, as is their custom. It was used thereafter as a sacred vessel on special occasions and as a ritual drinking-cup by their priests and temple officials." The Romans' grim accounts of human sacrifice were clearly designed to chill the hearts of Roman readers, and scholars might have taken them with a grain of salt except for the fact that they were later confirmed by archaeological evidence.

In total, these written accounts all create a rough outline of the Druids that seems to describe a pan-Celtic order of priests and political functionaries who performed rituals in oak groves using mistletoe. These accounts also suggest the Druids were central to sacred sacrifices, were keepers of a vast body of knowledge (including a calendar) through memorization, especially the theological concept of metempsychosis (the undeath of the soul and reincarnation). Druids also apparently served as neutral arbitrators and diplomats for the fractious Celtic chiefdoms. The ancient accounts are supported by the weak linguistic evidence that interprets the word "Druid" as originating from term meaning "those who know the oak" and "truth" in Old Celtic.

One of the most important observations that emerges from the Roman accounts is that the Druids had two distinct roles within society, making it all but impossible to completely understand their position among the ancient Celts. On the one hand, they were teachers, ritual leaders and scholars, keeping secret lore. This side is widely recognized in modern writings on the organization. However, the other side of the coin is that the Druids were the diplomats, arbiters and judges of their society, helping to keep the often precarious balance of power and peace between rival chiefdoms and factions in what must have been a complex political environment across ancient Gaul, Britain and Ireland.

---

40 An 'age' here is a roughly defined term, but it may refer to a larger cycle of events akin to the cyclical events in the Mesoamerican Long Count calendar. As the Druids apparently taught about the eternal, yet constantly renewing, nature of the earth, it is possible that Ages were seen as 'restarts' in the celestial cycles.
41 "Mesoamerican Writing Systems" at Ancientscripts.com, accessed online at: http://www.ancientscripts.com/ma_ws.html

In Gaul, the Druids' position was permanently weakened by the loss of their political power once the Romans subjugated the area and added it to the empire. Suetonius made it sound like stamping out the Celts was practically a moral imperative for the Romans, writing in the middle of the 1st century A.D., "Claudius destroyed the horrible and inhuman religion of the Gaulish Druids, which had merely been forbidden to Roman citizens under Augustus." Eventually, as the area was absorbed into the Roman Empire and forced to assimilate Roman religious institutions, the Druids were driven underground. Even still, the Roman emperor Aurelian consulted Druids in the late 3rd century A.D., as noted in *Aurelianus*: "On certain occasions Aurelian would consult Gaulish Druidesses to discover whether or not his descendants would continue to rule. They told him that no name would be more famous than those of the line of Claudius. And indeed, the current emperor Constantius is a descendant of his."

Despite this victory, Roman power in the region was short-lived, and in those areas of Britain that did not fall under Roman rule (especially Wales), the Druidic tradition appears to have actually lasted far longer than it did anywhere else. Caesar described the Druids as part of a tripartite division of intellectual labor, with diviners ("vates") and bards making up the other two legs of the tripod. Bards were singers and extemporaneous poets who performed in the courts of the rulers[42], and even after the Christianization of Wales, the Bardic tradition continued in the independent courts of the Welsh princes. As late as the 10th century A.D., a Welsh ruler named Hywel Dda ("Howel the Good")[43] drew up a document in Welsh listing the laws, duties and privileges of the bards, and all evidence points to them having taken up the political (if not religious) roles of the Druids, including moving between royal courts, interpreting laws, negotiating peace, and - in their role as genealogists - arbitrating on inheritance. Similar institutions existed in pre-colonization Ireland and the Gaelic-speaking areas of the Scottish Highlands as well.

Christianity

The history of the Celtic nations since the Roman invasion of Britain in 43 AD has often been told as one of conquest, oppression and resistance, with power emanating from southern and eastern capitals (London primarily, but also Paris, Dublin, Edinburgh and Cardiff) and dominating Celtic peoples of the north and west.[44] There is certainly some truth to that. Invasions, domination and centralization of power were all themes running through centuries of interaction between the Celts and others in the British Isles. Even those historians who doubt the reality of a Celtic culture recognize the domination of the British and French upon their

---

42 "Ancient Druids of Wales" at the homepage of the Museum of Wales, accessed online at: http://www.museumwales.ac.uk/en/rhagor/article/ancient_Druids/
43 "Hywel Dda" in the *Encyclopedia Britannica*, accessed online at: http://www.britannica.com/EBchecked/topic/273547/Hywel-Dda
[44]Such as Peter Berresford Ellis' numerous works like *Celt and Saxon: The Struggle for Britain AD 410-937* (1993) or *The Celtic Revolution: A Study in Anti-Imperialism* (2000)

peripheries.[45]

At the same time, this does not fully capture the dynamics of these long centuries, which included periods of long stability, times of Celtic resurgence, and even conflict amongst Celts[46] or Celts fighting alongside their supposed oppressors[47]. While the end result of the centuries was the compression of the Celtic languages to the westernmost fringes of their former territories and the political incorporation of Celtic peoples into centralized states, it should not be viewed as an epic or endless millennia-long struggle.

The story of the Anglo-Saxon conquest of Britain in the chaos of post-Roman Europe is told elsewhere. The Germanic tribes established their own kingdoms and displaced the native Brythonic-speaking Britons, some of whom seem to have conquered their own territories in modern-day Brittany. These small kingdoms warred against each other and against their Celtic counterparts, but they slowly consolidated and pushed back the Celtic leaders, leaving behind pockets of Celtic populations amongst the proto-English population. There is some evidence that there was an ethnic element to these wars, not only in the Arthurian legends on the Celtic side but also on the Saxon side, such as the reported ethnic cleansing of modern-day Exeter in 937 AD and the deportation of the Celts west of the River Tamar into modern-day Cornwall.

Meanwhile, there was a counter-invasion of sorts during the Middle Ages. The Catholic monasteries of Ireland (legendarily converted by St. Patrick in the 3rd or 4th century A.D.) sent out vast numbers of missionary priests, many of whom are today considered to be local saints in Cornwall, Wales and Brittany. These saints brought a distinctive brand of Christianity to western Britain and, along with it, a style of art called "Insular". This style of art descends from ancient La Tene designs, along with strong Scandinavian and Saxon influences. It is most famous in the legendary *Book of Kelis* kept today in Trinity College, Dublin[48].

---

[45] A famous example is Michael Hechter's classic 1975 work: *Internal Colonialism: The Celtic Fringe in British National Development*, published in Berkeley by the University of California Press.

[46] For instance, the famous feuds (in truth, small scale wars) between Scottish Highland Clans in the 16th - 18th centuries or the Irish Civil War from 1921-22.

[47] The most famous event being the Glencoe Massacre, when members of the Scottish Clan MacDonald were killed by members of Clan Campbell with aid from the government of William and Mary in London in 1692.

[48] "The Book of Kells" at the Website of the Library of Trinity College, Dublin. Accessed online at: http://www.tcd.ie/Library/manuscripts/book-of-kells.php

Illustrations of Matthew, Mark, Luke and John in the Book of Kelis

As the English consolidated their power, forming what would become the modern state of the United Kingdom, they not only conquered but also made concessions. Moreover, they never stamped out resistance to their rule. While the Celtic Nationalist Movement may have had some of its impetus in English (and French) Romantic projections, it also has roots in these longstanding desires for political and cultural autonomy in these regions. Irish nationalism in particular has long had a fiery tradition, and Scottish identity has been partially maintained through the continued existence of autonomous Scottish institutions. The Act of Union (1707) that bound Scotland and England with a single Parliament in Westminster allowed for Scotland to maintain a number of institutions, such as distinct Scottish courts and the Scottish Church, which was Presbyterian, not Episcopalian like the Anglican Church in England. These institutions have long helped to foster a sense of difference and have, in recent years, fueled demands for further autonomy. The Isle of Man has long maintained its own ancient parliament, the Tynwald, which is still able to hold the UK at arm's length at times. While not as well known as the Irish or Scottish causes, the Brythonic regions of Britain have also struggled for autonomy. This has been often tied up in the Welsh and Cornish preference since the 19th century for Nonconformist religious movements, especially Methodism.

That said, the process of "integration" was rarely peaceful. On numerous occasions, Celtic peoples, understanding that further centralization hurt their autonomy, fought in wider wars against centralizing powers. This was especially true in the Wars of the Three Kingdoms, a series of conflicts fought in England, Ireland and Scotland between 1639-1651 over questions of religion (Catholicism vs. Protestantism), government (Monarchy vs. Republic), and centralization (local peculiarities in law vs. single law codes). The most prominent of these conflicts was the three English Civil Wars, but they also include the Bishop's Wars (1639 and 1640) in Scotland, the Eleven Years War in Ireland (1641-1653) and the Scottish Civil War (1644-1651). These conflicts took on a deeply ethnic character, exacerbated English-Celtic conflicts, and strengthened the power of the central state in London[49].

These conflicts were followed by a restoration of the English Monarchy and the institution of the vehemently Protestant monarchs William and Mary in the "Glorious Revolution" of 1688, which set off another wave of conflict. This time, it was largely focused in the Scottish Highlands and Ireland as pro-Stuart (the Catholic-friendly family line displaced by William and Mary) "Jacobites" rose up in rebellion. The major rebellions occurred in 1715 and 1745, and their repression led to the destruction of the Scottish clan system and the Protestant Ascendancy in Ireland. The events of these wars are still celebrated by Northern Irish Protestants today in their yearly Twelfth of July festivals, celebrating King William's victory in the 1690 Battle of the Boyne. With a state hostile to their political aspirations and cultural traditions, the stage was set entering the 19th century for the large-scale repression of Celts, especially in rebellious Ireland and the Highlands. It was also out of this period, however, that Celtic nationalism appeared in its modern form.

While ancient sources described the Celts at length, the bulk of knowledge about Celtic mythology comes not from these early sources but from a series of medieval documents that relay the actual stories, flesh out the characters, and narrate the dramatic events. The ancient Celts had apparently known of writing - they used a script called Ogham which was said in Ireland to have been created by the god Ogma - but according to the Romans, the Druids refused to write down any sacred information, so the very existence of writing about Celtic mythology is remarkable and deserving of examination.

The greatest treasure trove of Celtic myth consists of documents written during the Middle Ages in Ireland and Wales. These documents are often (though not universally) short texts in medieval Welsh or Irish (also called Irish Gaelic), and some of these are spectacular works,

---

[49] *Soldiers and Strangers: An Ethnic History of the English Civil War* by Mark Stoyle (2005). Yale University Press.

such as the Red Book of Hergest[50] or the White Book of Rhydderch[51] (both from the 1300s), which contain not only myths but also poems, genealogies, and songs. These texts were written by learned monks in the languages that must have been their native tongues, and they show a profound mixture of Celtic and Christian religious and mythological worldviews. For instance, the Red Book is known for its "Triads," collections of three items with a similar theme. One Christian-based Triad (with a fair dose of Greco-Roman myth) is:

"Three Men Who Received The Might Of Adam:
Hercules the Strong, and Hector the Strong, and Samson the Strong. They were, all three, as strong as Adam himself."

Another Triad, clearly more influenced by older Celtic ideas, is:

"Three Great Enchantments of the Island of Britain:
The Enchantment of Math son of Mathonwy which he taught to Gwydion son of Dôn, and the Enchantment of Uthyr Pendragon which he taught to Menw son of Teirgwaedd, and the Enchantment of Rudlwm the Dwarf which he taught to Coll son of Collfrewy his nephew."[52]

In addition to the obviously non-Christian celebration of "enchantments," there is clearly an Arthurian reference (Uthyr Pendragon is often seen as Arthur's father) and a reference to the pre-Christian mother goddess Dôn.

The explosion of interest in ancient Welsh mythology during this period is not due to a growing interest in returning to pre-Christian religion; after all, the authors were undoubtedly men of deep Christian faith. Instead, they were probably connected to a growing sense of the importance of protecting Welsh identity. By the 1200s, the independent kingdoms of Wales were hard-pressed by the consolidating power of the English state to their east, leading to their final conquest and annexation in 1284. Upon the collapse of the Welsh courts, patronage for the traditional Welsh courtly life - especially bardic poems, songs and genealogies - suffered a fatal blow. Independent Wales had been a patchwork of small kingdoms (much like England before the conquests by Wessex) with a shared courtly culture, and this tradition was glued together by the "bards", a group of professional performers and historians with a shared guild-like organization and an elaborate system of training and credentialing.

These traditions were particularly ancient and had survived the destruction of the Druidic faith by Christianity through integrating the stories into the legitimacy of the Welsh kings. It appears that some of the Welsh-speaking Christian monks took it upon themselves to put these traditions

---

50 Oxford University, the current depository of the Red Book, has begun digitalizing it, and the results can be found here: http://image.ox.ac.uk/show?collection=jesus&manuscript=ms111
51 The National University of Wales, the current depository of the White Book, has a website dedicated to it, which can be found here: http://www.llgc.org.uk/index.php?id=whitebookofrhydderchpeniart
52 An extensive and often amusing collation of the Red Book's Triads can be found here: http://www.ancienttexts.org/library/celtic/ctexts/triads1.html

to paper in order to preserve some of the glory of the now-lost courtly world and protect threatened Welsh identity. This concern about the "Saxons" appears throughout the text, as with the Triad entitled the "Three Fortunate Concealments of the Island of Britain":

"The Head of Bran the Blessed, son of Llyr, which was concealed in the White Hill in London, with its face towards France. And as long as it was in the position in which it was put there, no Saxon Oppression would ever come to this Island."[53]

In Ireland and Scotland, there is a similar inheritance of medieval texts from the oral bardic tradition (with the more important bards being called "fili"). The bards of Ireland were not only highly trained but also inheritors of a long tradition, as they formed a caste into which one had to be born to participate. The bardic tradition in these areas suffered a similar fate to that in Wales, only slightly later, with the loss of political independence heralding the system's decline in 17th century Ireland and in the Scottish Highlands in the 18th century.

These texts lay largely dormant for centuries, collecting dust primarily in small family libraries in the noble houses of their respective nations, so it was only in the 18th and 19ths centuries that interest in ancient works began to rise in Britain and scholars (mostly amateur enthusiasts) began to comb ancient libraries for prizes. For instance, the famous Saxon poem Beowulf was only seriously examined for the first time in the late 18th century and published (in Latin) in 1815.

There were two scholarly and cultural trends during this period that led to this development. The first was the Romantic Movement, which included both a literary and scholarly enthusiasm for the Middle Ages. There was a turn away from the symmetrical Neo-Classical architecture and design and towards the Neo-Gothic, emulating cathedrals and buildings in the Tudor style. This was accompanied by a fascination with the lost and hidden and hopeless and fallen, including lost cities (like Machu Picchu or Troy) and hopeless causes (such as the famous Charge of the Light Brigade). In this context, there was a great interest in the Celts as both a lost civilization and a hopeless story, especially since it was largely (and incorrectly) believed that the Celtic languages would soon disappear forever.

The other trend that affected interest in this type of literature in the 19th century was the growing prominence of nationalism among Europeans. Across Europe, the old ties of empire and associated state churches were weakening as the subject peoples of Europe began to imagine themselves as parts of nations, groups of people who shared a language, traditions, folklore and a unique set of values and ways of viewing the world. Since many of these new nationalisms were not associated with the traditional languages of the courts, enthusiasts began to seek out ways of creating or (ideally) rediscovering a unique literary heritage, and for this reason, they often turned to either folk traditions or to surviving medieval texts. This led to

---

[53] *ibid*

works like the Grimm Brothers' famous collections of German folk stories, as well as the famous Finnish epic poem the Kalevala (composed of a pastiche of traditional songs). Before long, antiquarians were poring over ancient texts and finding such fundamentally important documents as The History of the Rus (a foundational text in Ukranian nationalism)[54].

In the Celtic countries, the search for texts took precedence over the collection of folk traditions, because the Welsh and Irish monks had provided an incredible wealth of documents to pore over. Perhaps the most important of the scholars working on this was Lady Charlotte Guest, who dedicated herself to Welsh manuscripts, particularly the Red Book and White Book. From 1838-1849, she worked to create a composite text called the *Mabinogion*. While there was nobody as influential as Guest in Ireland, this was a time when early Irish nationalists and scholars were digging into the rich inheritance of that land as well.

Lady Charlotte Guest

At the same time that true antiquarians like Lady Charlotte Guest were working hard to find the authentic remnants of the Celtic past, others sought to bolster the truth with their own creations. While fabrications of this type have haunted nationalist movements, the Celts have had two forgers of particular infamy: James Macpherson and Edward Williams. James Macpherson was an 18th century Scottish poet who published a cycle of epic poems called

---

[54] *The Cossack Myth: History and Nationhood in the Age of Empires* by Serhii Plokhy (2012). Cambridge University Press

Ossian, which he claimed were written by a blind bard of the same name. Macpherson even claimed Ossian was the son of Fionn mac Cumhaill, an important figure in Irish mythology. The tales, which told of tremendous tragedy and loss and were set in a land of mists and mystery, caught the imaginations of poets and readers across Europe and added fire to the incipient Romantic movement. Today, it is known that *Ossian* was a fabrication, but it continues to be a work of remarkable quality and imaginative power.

To the south, Welshman Edward Williams also sought to re-create ancient traditions while working in the late 18th century. Giving himself the bardic name Iolo Morganwg, he fabricated a series of medieval texts which claimed to document in great detail the religious rites of the ancient druids, as well as a series of new poetic forms he attributed to the great medieval Welsh bard Taliesin, who was already known for texts like the Book of Taliesin. Like Macpherson, his work continues to resonate today despite the fact he's a known fraud; the poetic forms he invented have been given widespread use, and his rituals are still used by Druidic organizations in Wales and beyond.

The Impact on Britannia

Modern knowledge of Irish mythology is the richest among all of the Celtic nations, probably because there was a tendency for pre-Christian mythological systems to be preserved better along the fringes of Europe[55]. The island's isolation, both geographical and cultural, meant that even though it eventually became staunchly Christian, its legends were maintained both in writing by monk-scribes but also in oral folklore.[56]

In ancient Celtic mythology, the theme of the permanence of both the soul and the universe itself, coupled with the cyclical nature of birth, death and rebirth, was explored, and one element of Irish tales is the repeated destruction and repopulation of the land. The Irish *Book of Conquests* tells how Ireland was repeatedly conquered by various peoples, and the text contains an extended list of these groups: the Partholons were conquered by the Fomorians, who were attacked by Nemeds. The Nemeds failed and were enslaved by the Fomorians, but then the Fomorians were conquered by the Fir Bolg, who were conquered by the Tuatha Dé Danann, who were conquered by the Milesians, who are the modern Irish[57]. While the Biblical Flood was integrated into the final cycle, the book is essentially pagan in nature and appears to echo the Druidic teachings about how life and the world are both simultaneously eternal and

---

55 For instance, the myths that make up the Finnish epic of the *Kalevala* (see *Kalevala Mythology Expanded Edition* by Juha Y. Pentikäinen [1987]) or the well-preserved Icelandic Epics such as the *Prose Edda* (see *The Prose Edda: Norse Mythology Penguin Edition* trans. and ed. by Jesse L. Byock [2005]) which survived as texts at the northern fringes of Europe.
56 *Irish Mythology* by George Townshend
57 "Fomorians" in the *Encyclopedia Mythica* (1999). Accessed online at:
http://www.pantheon.org/articles/f/fomorians.html

constantly cyclical.[58]

This text sets out the framework in which Irish myth takes place, though the two most recent conquests take the bulk of their content. The Tuatha were simultaneously a conquering (and eventually conquered) people of Ireland and also a race of gods who were venerated around the islands. So the myths center around tales of the war between the Tuatha and the Fir Bolg and then the interactions between the Tuatha and then of the coming of the Milesians and the acts of their kings and heroes (some of whom are related to the Tuatha).

Irish mythology is divided into a number of Cycles. A Cycle is a group of traditional stories, songs, poems and sayings which include overlapping characters and are seen as set in the same context. Classic examples from English literature are the stories of King Arthur or Robin Hood. For instance, the Arthurian Cycle includes not only full-length stories but also genealogies which include the High King, references to him in inscriptions, poems and triads. Some of these are quite minor, such as the Triad of the "Three Frivolous Bards of the Island of Britain" in the Red Book of Hergest, which reads, "Arthur, and Cadwallawn son of Cadfan, and Rahawd son of Morgant."

In order of occurrence, Irish mythology is divided into the Mythological Cycle (detailing stories of the gods and goddesses of Ireland), the Ulster Cycle (named after the northeastern province of Ireland, it details Ireland's Heroic Age, with godlike humans performing deeds of glory in a hazy period of the past), the Fenian Cycle (telling the tales of kings and warriors, particularly a band of warriors called the Fianna Éireann) and the Historical Cycle (the preserved songs of the court bards telling the events of the lives of kings)[59]. Many of these documents, along with more contemporary folklore, are preserved at the National Folklore Collection at University College Dublin[60].

Many of the tales of the Mythological Cycle have to do with the actions of the Tuatha Dé Danann, the "People of the Goddess Danu." This was a tightly knit pantheon of gods who were believed to have been related, regularly interacted with each other, and specialized in different areas of worship. Danu herself was the progenitor of the line as a matriarchal mother goddess, while her three eldest sons made up the primary deities of the pantheon: Dagda, Nuada, and Dian Cecht[61]. Dagda, whose name means "The Good God[62]," is associated with the earth and is the patron of treaties, life and death. He was married to The Morrigan, the triple goddess of battle, fertility and strife mentioned before, and her name translates to "Great Queen" or

---

58 Green = The Druids
59 *Pocket Dictionary of Irish Myth and Legend* by Ronan Coghlan (1985), Belfast: Appletree.
60 For the Collection's Website, visit: http://www.ucd.ie/folklore/en/
61 "Tuatha Dé Danann" by Micha F. Lindemans at the *Encyclopedia Mythica*. Accessed online at: http://www.pantheon.org/articles/t/tuatha_de_danann.html
62 Even today, "da" means "good" across the Celtic languages while a number of cognates similar to "dag" signify "God" such as "dia" in Irish, "dew" in Cornish or "duw" in Welsh.

"Phantom Queen." Their most important child was the goddess Brigid, who, like her mother, is a tripartite goddess with aspects dedicated to healing and fertility, smithing and fighting, and poetry and inspiration. Unlike the others, Brigid's immense popularity led to her continued appearance after Christianization; in Ireland, she was converted to St. Brigit, Jesus Christ's foster-mother, and on the island of Britain, her local form may have been converted to the Lady of the Lake, who granted King Arthur the legendary sword Excalibur.

Plate on a cauldron depicting Dagda.

Nuada, another child of Danu, was a similarly broad deity. Associated with the sun, the ocean, youth, beauty, poetry and warfare, he had a prominent role in the pantheon. His oceanic associations appear to be dominant, to the point that he was associated with Neptune by Roman observers. He also carried a mighty sword that would cut his enemies in half, and when he lost a hand in battle, his brother, Dian Checht, fashioned him a new one out of silver. Nuada was the King of Ireland, the grandfather of Cumhaill, and the great-grandfather of the legendary hero Fionn mac Cumhaill[63].

The final member of the three brothers was Dian Cecht, who was a god of healing and the physician of the gods. In addition to creating his brother's silver hand, he also created a blessed well called Slane where his fellow gods could bathe for healing when in battle[64]. He had six children, and one of his children, Cian (whose mother was also Dian Cecht's own mother Danu),

---

63 "Nuada" in the *Mythology Dictionary* (2014). Accessed online at: http://www.mythologydictionary.com/nuada-mythology.html
64 "Dian Cecht" in the *Encyclopedia Mythica* (1997). Accessed online at: http://www.pantheon.org/articles/d/dian_cecht.html

was the father of the god Lugh. Lugh was one of the most famous of the Tuatha, a god of light and the patron of every skill; he was worshiped during a long summer festival called Lugnasad and was associated with the Roman god Mercury. Other important gods included Lir, a sea god[65], and Ogma, the son of Danu and Dagda who is said to have invented the Ogham alphabet[66].

An engraving depicting Lugh

---

65 "Lir" in the *Mythology Dictionary* (2014). Accessed online at: http://www.mythologydictionary.com/lir-mythology.html
66 "Ogma" in the *Mythology Dictionary* (2014). Accessed online at: http://www.mythologydictionary.com/ogma-mythology.html

An illustration depicting Lugh and his magic spear.

As is common among the myths of many other peoples, the Celts not only told the stories of their gods but also of their human, or at least mostly human, heroes. The most famous of these are the stories of the Fenian Cycle. A number of mythological texts have come down from pre-Christian Ireland, but undoubtedly the most important of them is the Fenian Cycle, a collection of tales and songs (there is considerable overlap) about the deeds of the Fianna Éireann, a term which roughly translates into the "Warriors of Ireland." Fianna was a general term for bands of warriors and hunters held together by bonds of camaraderie who would wander the Irish countryside serving various nobles or living off of the land[67].

---

67 "Fenian Cycle" in *Britannica Concise Encyclopedia* (2009). Retrieved from
http://www.credoreference.com.libezproxy2.syr.edu/entry/ebconcise/fenian_cycle

The Fianna Éireann were led by the legendary figure Fionn mac Cumhaill - whose name is often spelled Finn MacCool in English. The adventures of Fionn and the Fianna are as complex, fantastical and contradictory as the old tales of King Arthur and the Knights of the Round Table. Many of these revolve around Fionn himself, and the Cycle is typically structured around the course of his life. Before his birth, his father was killed in battled by Goal Mac Morn, and the story of avoiding Mac Morn's wrath and then achieving his revenge serves as the overall framework of the Fenian Cycle. There are tales of Fionn's birth and how he was hidden away by his mother to protect him from Mac Morn, as well as how he spent a period of seven years of tutelage under the Druid Finegas. One day, Finegas caught the Salmon of Wisdom and had his student cook it, but when Fionn was accidentally burned by a bursting blister on the salmon, he sucked his thumb and received profound magical wisdom. With this knowledge, he assembled 150 of the High King's greatest warriors - the Fianna (also called the Fenians) - and launched his war against Mac Morn and his followers. Throughout his life, he was called to serve kings, defeat monsters like giants, fey folk and great wild hounds, and to defend his family[68].

---

68 "Finn MacCool" at the *Mythology Dictionary* (2012). Accessed online at: http://www.mythologydictionary.com/finn-mac-cool-mythology.html. "Finn Mac Cumhaill" at the *Encyclopedia Mythica* by Amy M. Durante (2001). Accessed online at: http://www.pantheon.org/articles/f/finn_mac_cumhail.html

An illustration depicting Fionn mac Cumhaill coming to the aid of the Fianna.

Despite the conversion to Christianity, the Irish and their Celtic brethren have never lost their fascination with Fionn and the Fianna. One of his first modern reappearances was when the 18th century Romantic poet James MacPherson borrowed the characters and themes from the Fenian Cycle to create his own mythological forgery: a set of epic poems attributed to Fionn's son Ossian (Oisín in Irish Gaelic). The work, entitled *Ossian*, was one of the most successful literary works of the time and, despite its relatively recent origin, continues to fascinate readers. Fionn also plays a crucial role in James Joyce's classic novel *Finnegan's Wake*[69].

---

[69] *Fionn mac Cumhaill: Celtic Myth in English Literature* by James MacKillop (1986). Syracuse, NY: Syracuse

More recently, anti-British militants in 19th century Ireland took up the name of the "Fenian Brotherhood," reveling in the masculine tales of warriors and defenders of the homeland that so strongly contrast with the widespread British propaganda about the feminized Celt[70]. Even today, the imagery continues; "Fenian" is a derogatory term for Catholic in Ulster and Glasgow, and images of Fionn sometimes appear in political murals in Belfast[71]. Outside of Ireland, the Fenian Cycle had an impact on tales among their ethnic cousins in Scotland and on the Island of Man.

The second major surviving Celtic mythological tradition originates from Wales. Similarly to the Irish tales, in Wales there is a diverse collection of stories that range from the purely mythological deeds of the gods to the heroic tales of humans and gods and monsters to the arguably historical deeds of kings and warriors that may be datable to historic events and archaeological sites.

Welsh myths had their own alternative names for the Celtic gods they shared with the Irish. The great goddess Danu was named "Dôn," and Lugh was called "Lleu," Lir had the Welsh name "Llyr", The Morrigan may have been related to "Modron" (who is also a possible origin for the Arthurian sorceress Morgan la Fay), and Nuada was called "Nudd." These gods were as similar to each other as the Greek and Roman gods; the names and some of the tales and associations differed slightly, but the similarities were obvious to any observer and the worshipers certainly understood them to be the same being.

University Press. See page 168.
70 *Celtic Identity and the British Image* by Murray G. Pittock (1999). Manchester University Press.
71 An example, taken by Simone Weil, can be seen here:
http://www.flickr.com/photos/57741776@N05/7593279962

An illustration depicting Llyr.

When it comes to Welsh mythology, the Mabinogion is central to it all. To create the *Mabinogion*, Lady Charlotte Guest combed all of the surviving medieval texts available to her at the time, from which she selected 11 tales. She not only chose the stories but also translated them from medieval Welsh, edited them for modern readers, organized them into chapters, and even named them. While impressive, this was not an altogether uncommon activity in her time, especially since Macpherson claimed to have done the same in Scotland, and there were similar projects with the story of Tristan and Isuelt and the Finnish mythic songs. Thus, despite their beauty and grandeur, the stories of the *Mabinogion* are not religious texts per se but instead a modern literary work created using source material that was similarly literary, not religious (despite being written by the Christians). One bias of the source material is that the tales are primarily about the acts of heroic humans, not gods or other events that violate Christian tenants such as the creation of the world.

The core of the *Mabinogion* consist four central stories known as the "Four Branches," which Guest argued were in fact all growing from the same "tree" of the original mythic source (presumably some epic Homeric-style Druidic poem). They primarily tell the story of the ancient Welsh kings, specifically a family called the Pryderi, and the many events that filled their rule. She also included three Welsh versions of Arthurian tales called the "Three Romances" and five other folktales, the most important of which is called the "Tale of Taliesin", which was about the most famous Welsh bard[72].

One of the more popular tales within the text is the story of "Culhwch ac Olwen" ("Kulhwch and Olwen" in English). Found in both the Red Book of Hergest and the White Book of Rhydderch, it tells the story of how young Culhwch defies his stepmother's attempts to seize his inheritance by marrying him to his stepsister. The spiteful stepmother tells Culhwch that he cannot marry anyone but Olwen, the daughter of a vile giant, but the giant is particularly opposed to the match because of a prophecy claiming that he will die if his daughter weds. When the giant is unable to kill Culhwch, he attempts to do away with the lad by proxy by sending him on 13 presumably impossible tasks and having him bring back 13 treasures to prove his love. Culhwch recruits his cousin, Arthur (the same King Arthur of the Round Table), and two of his cousin's knights: Kei and Gwalchmei (they would be the core of Sir Kay and Sir Gawain in later retellings). Luckily, before they do all of the tasks, Culhwch is able to kill the giant and marry Olwen[73].

---

72 For an online copy of the text in English, visit http://www.mabinogi.net/. "Pryderi," and "Pwyll" by Karen Davis in *The Encyclopedia Mythica* (1998). Accessed online at http://www.pantheon.org/articles/p/pryderi.html and http://www.pantheon.org/articles/p/pwyll.html

73 "Kulhwch and Olwen" at the *Encyclopedia Britannica* accessed online at: http://www.britannica.com/EBchecked/topic/324603/Kulhwch-and-Olwen

An illustration of Culhwch at Ysbadadden's court.

This text is basically a framework in which other stories are told, giving the teller flexibility to fit in stories that suited his or her fancy, and since the tale details many of the doings of Arthur and his men, it is also considered one of the earliest Arthurian legends. Important tasks include the hunt for the mighty boar Twrch Trwyth, the capture of the magical cauldron, and the rescue of one of Arthur's band, Mabon ap Modron, from prison. Mabon ap Modron is subsequently able to help them in their hunt for Twrch Trwyth, an epic battle in which many of Arthur's followers are slain[74].

---

74 A full text of *Culhwch and Olwen* can be found here:

Although these tales are about the acts of men, there are many echoes of earlier tales of gods. Mabon ap Modron may have been connected to the earlier Celtic god Maponos ("Great Son"), and in their quest to find him they must consult with the wisest animals, eventually learning of his whereabouts from a giant salmon (a similar theme to Fionn mac Cumhaill learning from the Salmon of Wisdom).

While legend says that Arthur was born at Tintagel Keep, a more accurate statement might be that Arthur and the Arthurian legend were born out of the imaginations, the fears and the dreams of the Celtic speaking peoples of western and southwestern Britain, those who are today called the Welsh and Cornish. Scholars refer to the earliest stage of Arthur literature as "Pre-Galfridian," with Galfridus being the Latin name for "Geoffrey". In other words, Pre-Galfridian literature consists of writings that existed before Geoffrey of Monmouth wrote *History of the Kings of Britain*. Today's scholars have five full manuscripts and 20 shorter texts which refer to Arthur, though many of these mention him only somewhat in passing. It's safe to assume that there were far more works that did not survive, and there were countless oral tales that were probably never recorded. Thus, most scholars assume these 25 works are the tip of an unknowable iceberg[75], and as such, the Arthurian Cycle is a collection of stories, songs, ceremonies and other texts that appear (and disappear) at different times in history.[76] Perhaps not surprisingly, some contradict each other outright, and others vary widely in style and message. These individual artistic pieces can be analyzed as myths on their own, but they also create a picture that can be taken as a whole.

The overarching myth in the Arthur Cycle is the story of the King himself. His birth is foretold famously by a young Merlin, who observes a battle between a red and white dragon that represent the Celts and Saxons respectively.[77] In some stories, he is then hidden away in the home of a knight named Sir. Ector until the "Call" is made explicitly and he withdraws the Sword in the Stone. He then becomes the King of Britain, bringing an era of peace, justice and respite from Saxon invasion through his court at Camelot until he is brought down by his own son, Mordred, who he sired due to the magical trickery of his half-sister Morgause. The High King does not die but is instead taken away to the Isle of Avalon to await being reborn when his people need him most. All of the elements of the Hero's journey are present: the Call, the separation, gifts from wise and powerful helpers (like Merlin and the Lady of the Lake),

---

http://en.wikisource.org/wiki/The_Mabinogion/Kilhwch_and_Olwen

75 "A Bibliographic Guide to Welsh Arthurian Literature" Accessed online at http://www.arthuriana.co.uk/notes&queries/N&Q1_ArthLit.pdf

76 In this case, "text" does not mean solely a written document but a wider definition which means any cultural performance or symbolic product. It could include not only written documents, but also works of art, rituals, musical performances, dances, public speeches, etc. This definition builds off of the work of anthropologist Clifford Geertz.

77 This story is commemorated even today in the Welsh flag, which bears a defiant red dragon. For more information, see http://welshflag.org/

challenges, and battle with his dark twin (his illegitimate nephew/son). His "boon" of good kingship is taken from the world until his return.

Of course, these are not the only tales woven into the Arthurian Cycle. While there are numerous small stories, the two other major arcs are the Betrayal of Queen Guinevere with Sir Lancelot, and the search for the Holy Grail, primarily by Sir Gawain and Sir Galahad. The tale of the Holy Grail is most explicitly a Hero's Journey, where the pure Galahad - enabled by the earlier boon of Arthur's court - is able to bring back the Holy Grail and restore Christ's love on Earth. Sir Thomas Malory cast Galahad as the ideal hero whose virtues are entirely due to his piety and chastity, and that theme was perpetuated by poets like Lord Tennyson, whose own Galahad states:

> "My good blade carves the casques of men,
>
> My tough lance thrusteth sure,
>
> My strength is as the strength of ten,
>
> Because my heart is pure…
>
> I never felt the kiss of love,
>
> Nor maiden's hand in mine."

George Frederic Watts' painting of Galahad

The Guinevere/Lancelot/Arthur tale is one of love, betrayal and suffering, and it is similar to another legend about Tristan and Isolde. Like in the story of the birth of Mordred, here Arthur is brought down not by force of arms but by betrayal, subterfuge and incest. The Guinevere-Lancelot story is not literal incest (and is thus not as destructive as the Mordred story), but it comes close since both figures have deep bonds to Arthur. Guinevere is his wife, and Lancelot is his brother-in-arms and was raised by Arthur's benefactor, the Lady of the Lake. It is the deep nature of the betrayal that gives the story much of its mythological power. One anthropologist of myth, Claude Levi Strauss, examined the taboo against incest, noting its universality in human societies and explaining how its appearance in myth serves to represent an inversion of the social order and typically presages the destruction of that same order.[78]

Herbert James Draper's painting of Guinevere and Lancelot

Furthermore, it can be argued that Arthur emerges as a "culture hero," or "a mythical or mythicized historical figure who embodies the aspirations or ideals of a society."[79] The earliest Arthur stories have him not as a king or enemy of the Saxons but as a wandering hero who embodies the best of what the Britons saw in men: bravery, generosity, loyalty to family, and physically vibrant. Fionn mac Cumhaill fulfills a similar role amongst the Gaelic peoples of Ireland, Scotland and the Isle of Mann. Where Arthur is the great mythical king, endowed with great powers but still mortal, of the Britons (especially the Welsh and Cornish), Fionn holds the same position amongst the western neighbors. In fact, the biggest difference between Fionn and Arthur is that the stories about Fionn simply didn't circulate as far or as much during the Middle Ages, ensuring that his story was less well-known. And since less was written about Fionn over the centuries, the legend didn't continue to build upon previous works, thus making Fionn's story less modern at the same time.

While Arthur may or may not have been based on historical figures, there are several characters that most certainly have mythological roots, particularly Morgan la Fey and the Lady of the Lake. Much speculation has been made about Morgan La Fey. The title "La Fey" literally

---

[78] *The Elementary Structures of Kinship* by Claude Lévi-Strauss, (1969), James Harle Bell and John Richard von Sturmer (trans.). Boston: Beacon Press.
[79] "Culture Hero" from the *Random House Dictionary*, 2013 edition

means "the Fairy," but in a time long before Tinkerbelle transformed popular images of them, fairies were powerful, mysterious, and otherworldly beings. What is agreed about Morgan is that she is a woman with magical powers who is deeply involved, though typically at a distance, with Arthur's reign. She sometimes aims to undermine him and sometimes seems more benign. The scholarly argument revolves around whether she was a creation of the Arthurian storytellers or whether she descends from a pre-Christian Celtic goddess (in Irish myth, the pre-Christian gods became known as the Fey after they were driven underground by the Humans). The most common argument is that she is the Welsh goddess Modron, but with her Breton name "Morgan." Less plausible but still possible is that she is a reference to the Irish war goddess Morrigan[80].

Like Morgan La Fey, the Lady in the Lake (who has many names) is most likely derived from ancient legends. The Lady's home in a kingdom under the waters of a magical lake, her gifts to the heroes Arthur and Lancelot, and her eventual presence on the boat that takes Arthur back to Avalon (hence her apparent immortality) all speak to her as more of a water-spirit or water-goddess than a woman. This has led some scholars to argue that she is a remnant of an earlier Celtic lake goddess.[81] Some have gone a step further and maintained that Morgan and the Lady are in fact aspects of the same goddess divided into two characters - one virtuous and one villainous - by later writers, but this argument is largely speculative.[82]

---

80 "Morgan La Fey: Celtic Origins" from the Camelot Project of the University of Rochester
  http://www.lib.rochester.edu/camelot/morgmenu.htm#Celtic
81 "The Lady of the Lake" http://www.britannia.com/history/biographies/nimue.html
82 "The Resurrection of Morgan le Fey: Fallen Woman to Triple Goddess" by Theresa Crater (2001), in the journal *Femspec* 3.1:12.

Howard Pyle's illustration of Morgan La Fay tossing Excalibur's sheath to the Lady in the Lake.

Along with Cai and Bedwyr, Arthur was also often accompanied by Gwalchmei, son of Gwyr. Gwalchmei is the son of Arthur's sister, and this character might be the prototype for Gawain, though this is not as easy to trace as the connections between Cai-Kay and Bedwyr-Bedivere.

The next major character is Medraut, the early Mordred. The nature of this character is a bit obscure, as "no source uninfluenced by Geoffrey of Monmouth or the Bruts makes Medraut Arthur's nephew or his betrayer/opponent -- in fact they seem rather to contradict these claims" making him a hero or a companion of Arthur.[83] Unlike Gwalchmei, who is specifically named as a kinsman of Arthur, no such connections are made for Medraut.

Uthyr Pendragon, who becomes Arthur's father Uther in later writings, also appears in the earliest writings. It is probable that he was thought of as Arthur's father or something of a magical Merlin-like figure who changes form and advises the hero.

Finally, this early tale included Gwenhwyfar, better known today as Guinevere, Arthur's wife. One of the prominent stories involving her has to do with her kidnapping by a villain named

---

[83] "Pre-Galfridian Characters" Accessed online at http://www.arthuriana.co.uk/n&q/figures.htm

Melway. After Arthur becomes a leader, his military campaigns, including a siege of Glastonbury, help win her back.

The tale of *Culhwch and Olwen* was preserved in a Welsh language collection called the Mabinogion, which was only translated into English by Lady Charlotte Guest in the 19th century. In the Mabinogion, Arthur is an overlord and a famed slayer of monsters. Arthur´s cousin Culwch requests his aid in winning the marriage of a beautiful giant named Olwen, who he is infatuated with due to a curse from his spiteful stepmother. Arthur sends his warriors (including Cai, Bedwyr and Gwalchmei), and Olwen´s father requests the completion of 40 impossible tasks (though the tale only recounts a few of them). This tale, however, largely serves as a frame for a long exposition of the heroic events in the life of Arthur, and lists of important persons. The most well-known event, which was recounted in other places as well, was Arthur's hunt of the great boar Twrch Trwyth. The direct links to oral traditions can be seen in this story: the recounting of long lists of ancestry was an important part of the bardic oral tradition, and the tale of Twrch Trwyth has direct links to other famous boars of Celtic lore. The great boar in the Mabinogion is similar to the Torc Triath in Ireland and the great Cornish sow Henwen, which gave birth to monsters fought by the Pre-Galfridian heroes. In fact, some legends claim Henwen gave birth to the cat-monster Cath Palug, which was killed by either Cai or Arthur, depending on the version.[84]

In these early stories, the picture of Arthur established by earlier sources is of a leader of a roving band of warriors. This band includes Cai, Bedwyr, Gwalchmei, Medraut and occasionally Uthyr, and the band wins glory, fights for treasure (such as a magical cauldron from Ireland), travels to the underworld, kills monsters, frees prisoners and protects the people of the land. In this form, they closely resemble other culture heroes, including the Irishman Finn Mac Cumhaill and his band of warriors, the Fenians. Arthur and his band are also depicted like the Irishman Cú Chulainn, and even the Greeks' Theseus.

Over time, however, this role of being the protector of the people would evolve from killing monsters to fighting the Saxons, the primary enemy of the Welsh and Cornish in the years after the fall of the Roman Empire. This transformation is easy to understand, regardless of whether Arthur was based on a historical figure or not. For example, it could be that there was a historical figure like Ambrosius to whom subsequent legends were attached, or it could be that there was simply an evolution in the mythological character of Arthur to suit new needs in cultural storytelling.

Perhaps the most important event attributed to this new Arthur was the victory at the Battle of Badon. Interestingly, the first reference to Badon is by the chronicler St. Gildas, who does not

---

[84] A translation of "Culwch ac Olwen" can be found here:
   http://www.ancienttexts.org/library/celtic/ctexts/culhwch.html;
   http://www.arthuriana.co.uk/notes&queries/N&Q1_ArthLit.pdf

mention Arthur but describes Ambrosius Aurelianus as the leader. He sets its date at 496 A.D. and describes how the victory in this battle halted the advance of the Saxons for a generation, guaranteeing the peace and survival of the Celtic peoples. Gildas is particularly important because he is the only person who wrote of the battle as having occurred in his lifetime. 496 was the year of his birth, but the events certainly would have been within memory of his parents' generation and make him the closest contemporary to them. The battle is also mentioned by the Venerable Bede in his *Ecclesiastical History of the English People* (731 A.D.), and he credits the victory to Ambrosius.

About 65 years later, the Welsh monk Nennius describes the battle and attributes it to Arthur in his *Historia Britonum* (circa 796 A.D.). Nennius also gives long descriptions of Arthur's campaigns against the Saxons. Furthermore, another similar source is the *Annales Cambriae*, which is dated to around 796 A.D. and written in the same manuscript as Nennius's work. *Annales Cambriae* elaborates on Arthur's role, and after these were published near the end of the 8th century, Ambrosius is no longer credited with the battle and it is always attributed to Arthur. It should also be noted that the battle is never mentioned in Saxon sources such as the *Anglo-Saxon Chronicle*, but this might be simply because it did not have the same importance when viewed from their eyes.[85]

There was another battle during this period that would become central to the Arthurian legend: the Battle of Camlann. In this battle, Arthur and Mordred face off, leaving Mordred dead and Arthur gravely wounded. The *Annales Cambriae* mentions this battle as having occurred in 537 and mentions that both men died, but not that they fought against each other[86].

Legends in Other Celtic Lands

The great literary traditions of Ireland and Wales provide the richest picture of Celtic mythology, and certainly the only ones with any breadth, but they are not the only Celtic countries, and mythology lives on in other areas of the Celtic world, typically in the form of folklore.

The Scottish Gaelic culture, including its myths, was part of the larger Irish cultural world. The clans of the Highlands had the same political systems, language, livelihood and mythology as their Irish cousins. Of particular importance were the stories of the Fenian Cycle; in fact, Fionn MacCumhail is said to have traveled to Scotland, creating the famous stone formation called the Giant's Causeway in northeastern Ireland as part of his bridge. His name is spelled "Finn" in Scottish or sometimes "Fingal", which was James Macpherson's interpretation of his name in his poem *Ossian*, but besides the respelling of their names (which is a modern

---

85 "The Battle of Badon" accessed online at http://www.lib.rochester.edu/camelot/badon/badnbibfrm.htm
86 A full text of the *Annals* can be accessed here: http://www.fordham.edu/halsall/source/annalescambriae.asp

phenomenon, as both traditions were largely oral), the Scottish versions are largely the same as their Irish counterparts.

Picture of the Giant's Causeway

While the English-speaking world typically thinks of Ireland, Scotland or Wales as Celtic countries, there is another Celtic land across the English Channel: the peninsula of Brittany. In Brittany, the descendants of migrants from Britain during the Middle Ages still speak a Celtic language called Breton. The Bretons, like the Irish, are a profoundly Catholic people, and much of their folklore revolves not around gods and heroes but instead around the events of the lives of the saints.

One important non-Catholic folkloric figure, however, is Ankou ("Death"). Taking a role similar to that of the Grim Reaper in English-speaking regions, Ankou is probably the direct descendant of ancient gods of death. He takes the form of either a skeleton or (more traditionally) the gaunt, pale body of the last person to die in the previous year. Ankou drives a cart around the Breton countryside collecting the souls of the dead and is associated with crossroads. He also takes the role of a psychopomp, a technical term for a being that accompanies the souls of the dead from the world of the living to their next destination. Ankou has even been integrated into Breton Catholicism and frequently appears carved into Breton churches[87].

A carved depiction of Ankou

Because of the relatively small size and close proximity of Cornwall to England and the center of English cultural power, the Celtic nation of Cornwall has suffered from the loss of the majority of its folklore, and no ancient texts survive bearing the stories of mythological beings

---

87 "Ankou" at the *Mythology Dictionary* (2012). Accessed online at: http://www.mythologydictionary.com/ankou-mythology.html. "Ankou" at the *Encyclopedia Mythica* by Amy M. Durante (2001). Accessed online at: http://www.pantheon.org/articles/a/ankou.html

or ancient heroes. There are a few surviving stories of spriggans, a local form of fairies, as well as knockers, spirits who make knocking sounds on the walls of tin mines.

The richest area of Cornish folklore is in the area of Arthuriana, as the Arthurian Cycle has always had a special relationship with the little peninsula of Cornwall. In Culhwch and Olwen, Arthur is said to have his court in Cornwall, and the ruined coastal castle of Tintagel on the north Cornish coast is said to have been his birthplace. Meanwhile, nearby Camelford claims to be the site of Camelot.

Remains of Tintagel Castle.

There are less place-based myths as well. Arthur appears battling Mordred and the Romans in a medieval mystery play *Beunans Ke* ("The Life of Saint Ke"), and there is an old belief that the choughs (a type of large raven and the national bird of Cornwall) serve as the eyes and ears of Arthur as he waits in Avalon to return to his people.

Like Scotland, the Isle of Man is a part of the larger Gaelic-speaking culture centered on Ireland. This little island has its own branch of the Gaelic language family and its own version of the Irish myths. The tales of the Fenian Cycle were told here too, with only minor changes to pronunciations of the names and details of the events. This serves as a reminder to avoid considering the written texts from Ireland as the most authentic original tales and these later retellings as corruptions or alternatives, because in any vibrant oral tradition, there are bound to be numerous local versions and these stories are also bound to shift over time to meet the needs of both tale-teller and audience. Thus, the Manx or Scotch versions are just as authentic as the old Irish manuscripts.

Beyond Fionn and the Fianna, the Manx have a rich tradition of ghost and monster stories, such as the Glashtyn, an aquatic goblin or water-horse (accounts vary) that turned into human form and seduced women from fishing villages. Another monster was the Buggane, an ogre-like beast with a tusked mouth who dwelt in tunnels around the island.

In some ways, despite the fact that the ancient Celts were the creators of these myths, learning anything about them from the stories is difficult because of the accumulation of centuries of additional material on top of them. What was added by medieval scribes? How had the myths changed in the mouths of the tellers in the centuries of Christian contact that occurred even before they were written down? Moreover, stories are not the same as theology, and this is just as true in the Celtic case as it is in the Christian or Muslim case. The story of Jonah and the Whale has theological implications, but they are not always easy to tease out of the story - hence the existence of professional theologians. With that in mind, what is available within the mythology that helps explain the Celts' belief systems?

To begin with, there is obvious evidence of a pan-Celtic pantheon of deities. Caesar, in describing the religion of the Celts, used his familiar gods but gave readers a picture of this diversity. The Celtic pantheon was diverse, and it is always difficult to know exactly which god Caesar meant when he wrote "Mercury" or "Mars," but his statement is a first step for further insights. In the following quote from *The Gallic Wars*, Irish names have been substituted for the original Latin, and the Welsh and Gaulish and other cognates are noted in the footnotes[88]: "Among the gods, they most worship Lugh[89]. There are numerous images of him; they declare him the inventor of all arts, the guide for every road and journey, and they deem him to have the greatest influence for all money-making and traffic. After him they set Oenghus[90], Tuireann[91], Dagda[92], and Brigid[93]. Of these deities they have almost the same idea as all other nations: Oenghus drives away diseases, Brigid supplies the first principles of arts and crafts, Dagda holds the empire of heaven, Tuireann controls wars. To Tuireann, when they have determined on a decisive battle, they dedicate as a rule whatever spoil they may take. After a victory they sacrifice such living things as they have taken, and all the other effects they gather into one

---

88 "The Celtic Gods" in the *Encyclopedia Britannica* accessed online at:
   http://www.britannica.com/EBchecked/topic/101803/Celtic-religion/65539/The-Celtic-gods
89 Mercury, Lleu in Welsh, Lugus in Gaul
90 Apollo, Maponos in Gaul, Mabon in Wales
91 Mars, Taranis in Gaul, Thor among the Norse
92 Jupiter, Zeus in Greece, Sucellus in Gaul
93 Minerva, Sulis in Gaul, Athena in Greece

place."

In many ways, the gods here are more similar to the Catholic conception of saints than they are to the Christian God, because they are patrons of particular places and professions, they can be appealed to, and they can even be bribed with sacrifice. The cyclical nature of the Celtic understanding of the universe holds all things, including both the gods and the universe itself, as both eternal and cyclical. Hence, the gods rose up at a particular time in the past and will fall again, only to rise up in new forms - much like the many conquests of Ireland in *Book of Invasions*. This also meant that the dividing line between humans and gods was blurrier than in the Judeo-Christian tradition, especially since ostensibly human heroes like Fionn MacCumhail had divine blood and performed feats beyond the abilities of mere men. In fact, the Romans attributed the near-suicidal bravery of the Celts in battle to their belief in their coming rebirth. Examination of the myths, especially the tales of Fionn MacCumhail and the Fianna, show that bravery and personal skill at arms was highly favored, as was a disregard for the lives of warriors. At the same time, the Celts did not believe their lives were governed by Fate, a belief that was so widespread in both Norse and Greek myth.

The tales of the great Celtic heroes can be seen not only as representations of a distinctive Celtic theology but also as examples of archetypal mythical heroes. For the better part of a century, scholars have shown that the world's many mythological heroes share certain traits and perform a similar psychological role. Joseph Campbell, in his seminal work *Hero of a Thousand Faces*, argued that the world's heroes were manifestations of a single "monomyth." This story, ostensibly about the journeys and adventures of a heroic individual, were in fact elaborate metaphors for the journey of the human soul over the course of their life from birth to enlightenment to death. Campbell noted how the hero is marked at a young age and removed from normal society, then sent on a "Quest", during which he experiences a "Call", a message requiring him to save his people. He gathers up aid and wisdom and overcomes numerous challenges before finally facing his ultimate foe and overcoming it. With the salvation of the world now in his hand, something called a "Boon", he returns back to society and restores it.

The great Celtic myths fit within this pattern. For instance, the tales of Fionn MacCumhail show the path of a Hero, and due to the nature of a Cycle, composed as it is of many disparate songs and stories, no single tale tells the full account of the hero's life. Moreover, some of the stories may not fit into the overall arc of the Quest story. The "Call" for Fionn is the unjust murder of his father, which forced him to be set apart from society and be raised in secret. He is then trained by the wise druid, where he encounters the Salmon of Wisdom, thus gaining the tools he needs to become the Hero. He gathers his allies around him and sets about battling various foes. While he does eventually set the world right again by avenging his father's murder, his entire story is about the defense of society from the monstrous forces that menace it. Through courage, loyalty and force of arms, the Fianna overcome all forms of enemies and fulfill the role of the Hero.

While there are undoubtedly local elements worked into this story, the myth resonates with the reader in large part because of its universal character and the way that it speaks to the long-term struggle of humanity. It is this capability of relating to the human Hero that makes the heroic cycles so popular and long-lasting compared to the Cycles that deal with the doings of the inhuman gods. It is in part because of this that these stories were preserved and passed from person to person for so many centuries, eventually arriving to the modern period in the form of the Arthurian Cycle or the Fenian Cycle. Understandably, by dealing with such human themes, even these old stories can continue to inspire the imaginations of millions.

Celtic Heritage

The modern appreciation of the Celts continues to grow as more and more people discover more about the past. Leprechauns, the wearing of green on St. Patrick's Day, Celtic music, interest in protecting nature, a fascination of the cultural shifts of the past, the growing appeal of matriarchy, and looking at the ways of life from other perspectives all contribute to the fascination with the Celts.

Naturally, some people have turned to the ancient Celts as a source of nationalist inspiration. Perhaps one of the most famous is Queen Boudica of the Iceni tribe in Britain during the 1st century CE. She was a legendary figure who believed very strongly in Celtic myth.

Prasutagus had been Boudica's husband and king. Together, they had two daughters, and throughout the king's later years, he had held his title as a sovereign ally of Rome. In his will, he had left the kingdom to the joint custody of his daughters and the emperor. But the Romans ignored his wishes. After he had died, the Romans took his property as their own.

The Roman historian Tacitus wrote that the soldiers flogged Boudica and raped her daughters. Around 60 CE, Boudica led her tribe and several others in revolt against the treacherous Romans. While launching the attack, she called upon the Celtic goddess, Andrasta, to guide them to victory. The Celtic Briton tribes annihilated what is today Colchester.

When the Roman governor, Gaius Suetonius Paulinus, heard of the attack, he hurried to what his intelligence sources told him would be the next target: Londinium, a small community which had been in existence for only about two decades. Without the necessary resources to defend the future London, the governor had all the citizens evacuate.

After defeating a portion of the Legio IX Hispana, Boudica's army burned both Londinium and nearby Verulamium. They slaughtered nearly 80,000 Roman citizens and native Britons.

The Roman governor reorganized his legions, and despite being outnumbered, defeated the Iceni and their confederates. Boudica died not long afterward.

Though she lost her battle against the Romans, she has since become a symbol and national heroine for all who struggle to obtain justice and liberty.

Though the Celts appeared to be nominally patriarchal, they were far more egalitarian than the Greeks or the Romans. In this, they were far more like the Etruscans and Basques. When Queen Boudica took her tribe to war against the Romans for their betrayal, treachery, and rape of the Iceni princesses, she showed a strength of character that transcends gender. And with the Tuatha Dé Dannan literally named after the goddess who led them, rather than being named after her husband, we might wonder if the Celts had a matriarchal past.

In his book, *Mission: Atlantis,* researcher and science writer Rod Martin, Jr., explored the possibility that many of the ancient tribes of Europe may have been, at one time, matriarchal. The Basques of northern Spain and southern France speak an agglutinative language isolate, as did the Etruscans of northern Italy. Martin pointed out that what are perhaps the two most sentimentally favorite words in any language are "father" and "mother," and that the pattern of these words across numerous language isolates reveals an interesting pattern.

Both the Basques and the Etruscans have a history of more egalitarian societies. The Basque word for mother is "ama," while the word for father is "aita." Curiously, the same words in Etruscan seem swapped, with mother being "ati" and father being "apa." Both "ati" and "aita" are similar, while "ama" and "apa" use a labial sound in between two short vowels. This, by itself does not say much, but the Etruscan pantheon reveals something a bit more intriguing. The Etruscan goddess of beginnings, you may remember from earlier in the book, was named "Ana," while her counterpart, the god of endings, was named "Aita." Basque for mother ("ama") is very similar to the Etruscan goddess of beginnings ("Ana"), while the Basque for father ("aita") is the same as the Etruscan god of endings ("Aita"). Could the Etruscan roles have been swapped in the past, but the words stayed with the roles rather than the genders? Could it be that in pre-history, the Etruscans were matriarchal, perhaps like the Basques? In earlier times, it may have been that mothers were the rulers, and when the society changed to patriarchy, men became the new "mothers."

A similar thing may have happened in Georgian society (Caucasus, at the eastern end of the Black Sea), also quite egalitarian. Georgian is also an agglutinative language isolate. The word for mother in Georgian is "deda," while the word for father is "mama." It also remains curious that the 19th century linguists thought Georgian and Basque showed great affinity with one another. So, taken with this fact, they even named the region around the myth of Colchis, the Golden Fleece, and the golden dragon that guarded it, to be "Iberia," just like the region of Spain and Portugal.

The Celtic goddess Danu may yet be another clue to a matriarchal past. Though there are no legends that specifically mention her, modern scholars have derived her importance through implication: the naming of the tribe of gods after her, and the naming of other important locations in her honor, including, it seems, the River Danube. Though this notion has its critics, it remains a possibility.

Further Reading

Aldhouse-Green, Miranda (1997). Exploring the World of the Druids. London: Thames and Hudson.

Chadwick, Nora (1966). The Druids. Cardiff: University of Wales Press.

Collis, John. The Celts: Origins, Myths and Inventions. Stroud: Tempus Publishing, 2003.

Cunliffe, Barry. The Ancient Celts. Oxford: Oxford University Press, 1997.

Ellis, Peter Berresford (1994). The Druids. London: Constable. ISBN 978-0-09-472450-1.

Herm, Gerhard. The Celts: The People who Came out of the Darkness. New York: St. Martin's Press, 1977.

Hutton, Ronald (1991). The Pagan Religions of the Ancient British Isles: Their Nature and Legacy. Oxford: Blackwell. ISBN 0-631-18946-7.

Hutton, Ronald (2007). The Druids. London: Hambledon Continuum.

Hutton, Ronald (2009). Blood and Mistletoe: The History of the Druids in Britain. New Haven, Connecticut: Yale University Press. ISBN 0-300-14485-7.

Maier, Bernhard: Celts: A History from Earliest Times to the Present. University of Notre Dame Press 2003.

Piggott, Stuart (1968). The Druids. London: Thames and Hudson.

Powell, T. G. E. The Celts. New York: Thames and Hudson, 1980. third ed. 1997.

Raftery, Barry. Pagan Celtic Ireland: The Enigma of the Irish Iron Age. London: Thames & Hudson, 1994.

Ross, Anne (1967). Pagan Celtic Britain. London: Routledge.

Rutherford, Ward (1978). The Druids and their Heritage. London: Gordon & Cremonesi. ISBN 978-0-86033-067-7.

Printed in Great Britain
by Amazon